T0279342

SECRET
DUBLIN
AN UNUSUAL GUIDE

Pól Ó Conghaile

JONGLEZ PUBLISHING

Travel guides

Pól Ó Conghaile is a travel writer based in Dublin. He is Travel Editor at *The Irish Independent* and Independent. ie, and a regular contributor to *National Geographic Traveller* as well as national TV and radio in Ireland and the UK. He has been named Irish Travel Journalist of the Year several times and the British Guild of Travel Writers 'Travel Writer of the Year'. Pól travels all over the world, but his favourite city – and return destination – remains the same: Dublin. Follow Pól on Twitter at @poloconghaile, or visit poloconghaile.com

We have taken great pleasure in drawing up *Secret Dublin – An unusual guide* and hope that through its guidance you will, like us, continue to discover unusual, hidden or little-known aspects of the city.

Descriptions of certain places are accompanied by thematic sections highlighting historical details or anecdotes as an aid to understanding the city in all its complexity.

Secret Dublin – An unusual guide also draws attention to the multitude of details found in places that we may pass every day without noticing. These are an invitation to look more closely at the urban landscape and, more generally, a means of seeing our own city with the curiosity and attention that we often display while travelling elsewhere ...

Comments on this guidebook and its contents, as well as information on places we may not have mentioned, are more than welcome and will enrich future editions.

Don't hesitate to contact us:
• Jonglez Publishing,
  25, rue du Maréchal Foch
  78000 Versailles, France
• Email: info@jonglezpublishing.com

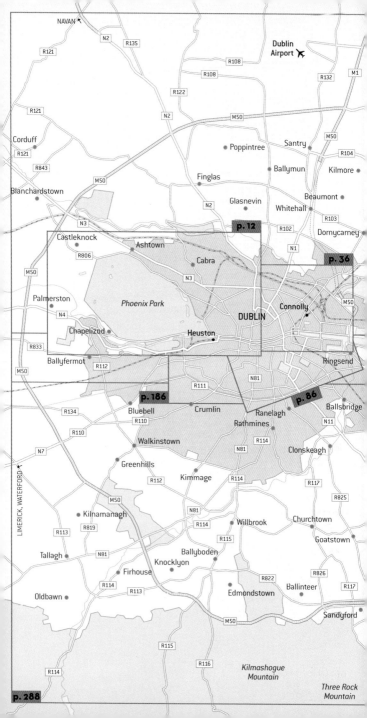

R107
Kinsaley
Portmarnock
R124
R106
R123
R106
N32
Darndale
R809
Donaghmede
Baldoyle
Ireland's Eye
R107
Edenmore
R104
Kilbarrick
Sutton
R105
Howth
Coolock
R105
Artane
Raheny
R107
R105
Saint Anne's Park
Clontarf
Dollymount
R807

Sandymount

Merrion
R118
Booterstown
Blackrock
N31
N31
Dun Laoghaire
Mount Merrion
N11
Monkstown
R119
Kilmacud
Deansgrange
Sallynoggin
Dalkey
R113
R827
R828
R118
Dalkey Island
Cornelscourt
Killiney
M50
N11
R119
R118
R117
Carrickmines
Ballybrack

WICKLOW, WEXFORD ↘

N

0   500   1 000 m

CONTENTS

Phoenix Park & Quays

Centre North

Centre South

CONTENTS

Wood Quay to War Memorial

Outside the Centre – North

Outside the Centre – South

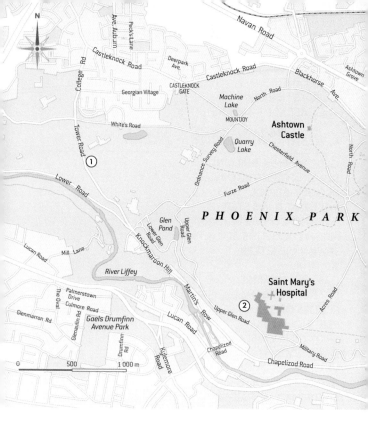

Phoenix Park & Quays

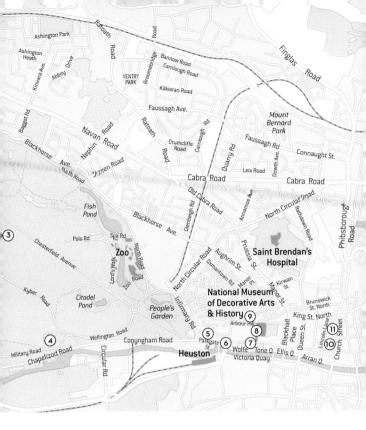

CLOCK TOWER, FARMLEIGH

Mister Guinness has a clock ...

Farmleigh House & Gardens, Phoenix Park, Dublin 8
01 815-5914
farmleigh.ie
Daily 10am–6pm (last admission 5pm)
Admission: free
Dublin Bus stop 1670 is at the Castleknock gate to Phoenix Park. The 37 from
Baggott Street (via Suffolk Street) stops here (15-min. walk)

Farmleigh is a 51-hectare estate cocooned within the Phoenix Park. Developed over several decades by Edward Cecil Guinness (Lord Iveagh, 1847–1927), the house and gardens were bought by the Irish government in 1999 and have since hosted Queen Elizabeth II and Emperor Akihito of Japan, among other official visitors. Wildly eclectic interiors, a Dutch-style sunken garden, a Boathouse Café and an art gallery are all open to the public, but the most unusual feature of all, perhaps, is the Victorian Clock Tower.

> *Mister Guinness has a clock*
> *And on its top a weathercock*
> *To show the people Castleknock*

So goes a local ditty celebrating the 37m landmark, which can also be spotted by eagle-eyed drivers passing across the West Link toll bridge. The tower is said to have been the work of the Guinness Brewery's engineering department, and its east and west faces both bear clocks adorned with cast-iron dials and copper hands. Surprisingly, however, the 'Clock' Tower also contains an 8,183-litre water tank. Hidden away at balcony level, this tank once provided a private water supply for the estate, pumped via a weir built into the River Liffey at the Strawberry Beds, a mile-long (1.6 km) millrace, and a turbine that both pumped water and generated electricity for Farmleigh. The bridge that was constructed to carry the lines over the river can still be seen – albeit in a dilapidated state – near the Angler's Rest pub.

The Clock Tower is reached via the pathways leading south-east from the house. Short, steep steps lead through a sumptuous series of mature trees towards its base and a doorway topped by a granite stone into which the date '1880' has been carved. Views from the balcony are said to be breathtaking, stretching as far as Malahide to the north and the Dublin Mountains to the south, although it was closed when Secret Dublin paid a visit. The clock has remained in perfect working order since it was assembled by the celebrated Sir Howard Grubb, who also provided the instrumental equipment for the great roof at Dunsink Observatory. Today, however, its weights are raised electrically.

KNOCKMAREE DOLMEN

A prehistoric tomb in Phoenix Park

Phoenix Park, Dublin 8
phoenixpark.ie
Open 24/7, year-round
Dublin Bus stops 2195 and 2247 are at the Chapelizod Gate to St Mary's
Hospital: routes 25, c5 and c6 serve the stops. Knockmaree dolmen is about 500
metres up the Upper Glen Road (10 mins)

O f all the sights to stumble across in this richly layered city, a little dolmen is surely one of the most surprising. Yet here it is. Sitting just west of St Mary's Hospital, by a small lodge atop of the hill of Knockmaree, is a squat prehistoric burial chamber said to be between 4,500 and 5,500 years old.

That's an extraordinary age – if it's the older end of that range, as the Phoenix Park website suggests, then the structure is of similar vintage to the passage tombs of Newgrange and Knowth, and could be older than Stonehenge. It's also thousands of years older than the park in which it sits, and a great piece of perspective – this giant enclosure feels like it has always been here, but in the great context of time, it's really just a babe. As, of course, is Dublin itself.

Despite all that, Dublin's dolmen (or more correctly, a cist grave) is a relatively modest discovery. Follow the trails up the hill after the sign for Cara Cheshire House, and you'll find small slabs supporting a coffin-shaped capstone of just under 2 metres in length, said to have come from the nearby River Liffey. You can't see into any chamber, but records suggest it measures roughly 1.2 metres in length by 0.6 metres in width. The tomb was discovered in 1838 by workmen removing an ancient tumulus (or mound), with 'skeletons, pottery and other relics' such as jewellery made from shells discovered inside (these are now held in the National Museum). 'The heads of the skeletons rested to the north, and, as the enclosure is not of sufficient extent to have permitted the bodies to lie at full length, they must have been bent at the vertebrate, or at the lower joints', according to a report by the Royal Irish Academy, which carried out the site survey.

There's no protection around the stones, and it's often dotted with rubbish. The laissez-faire attitude isn't a new development, either. Writing in his *Handbook of Irish Antiquities* a decade or so after the discovery, William F. Wakeman took a moment to gently chide passers-by for defacing it. In his work, he wonders how long it should 'remain a prey to every wanderer in the Park desirous of possessing 'a piece of the tomb' in order to shew it as a wonder'.

PHOENIX PARK MURDER VICTIMS' ③ MEMORIAL

Dublin's most discreet memorial

Phoenix Park, Dublin 8
01 677-0095
phoenixpark.ie
Phoenix Park is open 24/7, year-round
Admission: free
Transport: Luas, Heuston (Red line; 25-min. walk); Dublin Buses 25 and 26 stop near Parkgate Street (main gate entrance), Islandbridge turnstile and Chapelizod Gate

The murders may have scandalised society, but the spot is subtly marked. So subtly, in fact, that it took this writer three attempts to find it. Even then, the modest white pebble cross, cut into the grass and covered in autumn leaves, could only be pinpointed with the help of a very obliging park employee.

Persistence pays off, however. The cross, less than a metre in length, is located on Chesterfield Avenue, almost directly across from the park's 'vista' of Áras an Uachtaráin, the President's official residence. Scanning the grass verge between the road and the cycle lane, you'll find it roughly 12m north-west of a battered old distance marker. The first thing that strikes you are the little white stones. The memorial may be tricky to locate, but it is obviously being maintained … signalling the historical significance of the site, almost a century and a half since those tragic events.

What happened here? On 6 May 1882 the Chief Secretary for Ireland, Lord Frederick Cavendish, was walking through the park with the Permanent Undersecretary, Thomas Henry Burke. Cavendish was on his first day in the job. As they passed the then Viceregal Lodge, the pair were ambushed by members of rebel nationalist group 'The Invincibles' and stabbed to death with surgical knives. Burke was the target (Ireland's most senior civil servant was resented for his association with coercive policies towards tenant farmers under the previous Chief Secretary, 'Buckshot' Forster); Cavendish was the collateral damage.

The murderers escaped in a horse-drawn cab, but their flurry of violence had reverberations throughout Irish history. Britain and Ireland were scandalised, the press had a field day, and despite wide condemnation (including that of Charles Stewart Parnell, leader of the Irish Home Rule Party in the British House of Commons), the killings contributed to the break-up of the British Liberal Party and a decades-long setback for Home Rule. Ultimately, five men were hung at Kilmainham Gaol for the crime; others convicted as accessories.

The discreet cross – a memorial to the victims, rather than the killings, of course – has been the subject of some intrigue over the years, but over time has been taken under the care of the Office of Public Works (OPW), who quietly maintain it without any explanatory plaque or markings.

MAGAZINE FORT

Dublin's only remaining fort

Phoenix Park, Dublin
phoenixpark.ie
Open 24/7, year-round
Admission: free
Dublin Buses 25 and 26 stop at the Chapelizod Gate, Parkgate Street and the
Islandbridge Turnstile, which are closest to the magazine fort

Phoenix Park is one of the largest enclosed recreational spaces of any European capital and there's no shortage of things to do within its 1,752 acres: Dublin Zoo, Farmleigh House & Estate, Áras an Uachtaráin and Ashtown Castle are all located here. Hidden away in the south-east of the park, however, is a more unusual attraction. Here, sunk into the hilltop site where Sir Edward Fisher built the original Phoenix Lodge in 1611, you'll find the decaying remains of a magazine fort. It dates from 1734, when the Duke of Dorset directed that a powder magazine be provided for Dublin: Fisher's Lodge was knocked down and the star-shaped structure was installed in its place.

The fort's dubious merits drew a stinging satirical response from Dean Jonathan Swift, who was inspired to whip out his notebook after encountering the building. 'Behold, a proof of Irish sense', he wrote.

'Here Irish wit is seen; when nothing's left that's worth defence, we build a magazine.' The words are said to be the last Swift ever wrote, though they did little to stop the development. In 1801 an additional wing was added to the fort to accommodate troops.

The magazine fort has seen some action, though not the kind for which it was intended. Irish Volunteers captured it during the Easter Rising of 1916 and the IRA raided the Irish army's stocks here on 23 December 1939. The so-called 'Christmas Raid' saw more than 1 million rounds removed from the fort in over a dozen lorries – though the audacious heist was followed by a disastrous aftermath (for the IRA, at least). Several arrests were made, most of the ammunition was recovered and an outraged Dáil voted to extend a new Emergency Powers Act to provide for the internment of Irish citizens at detention camps in the Curragh.

In recent years, access to the fort's interior was forbidden due to its instability, but the Office of Public Works (OPW) now has plans 'to conserve the fort and to open it as an exciting new interactive visitor experience' in years to come. Rampart and moat walks are also proposed. Until then, visitors can still follow a trail around the earthen defences that echo its star-like shape. At their sharpest points, the outer walls look almost like the prows of ships, and the tall, redbrick chimneys seem to play on the Wellington Monument beyond.

'BONGO' RYAN'S BOOTH

A vessel of Victoriana

Ryan's, 28 Parkgate Street, Dublin 8
01 677-6097
thebuckleycollection.ie
Monday–Thursday 12pm–11.30pm, Friday & Saturday 12pm–12.30am,
Sunday 12.30pm–12am.
Luas, Heuston (Red Line; 5-min. walk); Dublin Bus stops 1474 and 7078 are
nearby on Parkgate Street

Dublin has its vessels of Victoriana, but few follow through with the level of detail and deliciousness on display at Ryan's of Parkgate Street. Established in 1886, the pub's oak and mahogany bar, antique engraved mirrors and tantalising snugs – hidden behind mirrored partitions towards the rear of the premises – are just the entrées.

Look out for the old gas lamps on the counters, clutching their orbs of light with artistry and elegance. Or the tiny brass match lighters fixed to counters and windowsills throughout the pub. In years gone by, punters would have struck matches against these as handily as they struck up conversations with each other, and one can only imagine the fug of smoke drawing down over the mirrors and mahogany. There are brass foot rails, tobacco drawers, whiskey casks, and the snugs even have little bells for summoning the barmen. These whispery little booths date back to an era when it was frowned on for a lady to enter a pub, but their privacy also appealed to passing priests and policemen. Today, they're listed by Dublin City Council and have been booked over the years by U2, among others.

Best of all is the booth once occupied by Willie 'Bongo' Ryan. Set right in the heart of the mahogany bar, this is where the Limerick man sat taking money from, and issuing change to, his barmen. It's a plum spot and the endless mirrors must have enabled him to keep an eye on every nook and cranny of his bar. Above the booth, a mechanical clock burrows right through the woodwork. Made in Germany, it's said to be the oldest two-faced indoor clock in the country, and 'Bongo' traditionally set it five minutes fast, allowing his patrons a few precious moments of grace before catching their trains out of Heuston station.

Today, those patrons are likely to be lawyers from the nearby Criminal Courts of Justice, GAA (Gaelic Athletic Association) fans wetting their beaks before a match at Croke Park, diners enjoying a swift aperitif before repairing to the steakhouse upstairs, or the odd tourist, delighted to have stumbled across this Victorian time warp. Step inside, delight in the detail and lament the fact that the snugs are taken. It's like a visit to Dublin, c. 1886 – all that's missing is 'Bongo' himself.

ANNA LIVIA

The Floozy in the Jacuzzi

Croppies Memorial Park, Wolfe Tone Quay, Dublin 8
dublincity.ie
December & January 10am–5pm, February & November 10am–5.30pm,
March & October 10am–6.30pm, April & September 10am–8.30pm, May &
August 10am–9.30pm, June & July 10am–10pm
Luas, Heuston (Red Line; 5-min. walk); Dublin Bus stops 1474 and 7078 are
nearby on Parkgate Street

Dublin has erected its fair share of controversial public artworks, but Éamonn O'Doherty's *Anna Livia* may well have been the most controversial of all. Commissioned by Michael Smurfit for the Dublin Millennium celebrations of 1988, the statue was embedded in the middle of a busy pedestrian island on O'Connell Street and rapidly became a focal point for praise, ridicule, mischief and anti-social behaviour in equal measure.

Anna Livia, 18 ft (5.5 m) long and reclining in a gushing fountain, was designed to symbolise the River Liffey (her name evokes Anna Livia Plurabelle, a character fulfilling a similar function in Joyce's *Finnegans Wake*). The artistic merits of the bronze figure were not obvious to all, however, and as is their wont, Dubliners soon brought her down to earth with a nickname – 'the Floozy in the Jacuzzi'. Over time, Gardaí and City Council workers despaired of the hoards of people cavorting on the fountain's edges, the constant stream of litter tossed into its water, the baths taken during sunny spells, and the foam parties whipped up whenever someone emptied a bottle of washing-up liquid into the mix. *Anna Livia* was finally removed during the redevelopment of O'Connell Street in 2001, replaced by the more masculine *Dublin Spire* ('the Stiletto in the Ghetto') and dispatched into storage at St Anne's Park in Raheny.

Unbeknown to many, however, this sculpture has since experienced a second coming. In 2011 *Anna Livia* was taken out of storage and transported down the Liffey on a barge to her new home in Croppies Memorial Park. This small, flowery triangle at the intersection of Benburb Street and Wolfe Tone Quay was formerly part of the military recreation grounds at Collins Barracks, and as a public park, measures barely 0.25 hectares. O'Doherty's sculpture has been lowered into position in a curvy, ornamental pond and, with the odd duck for company, looks currently to be enjoying a very relaxed retirement.

THE CROPPIES ACRE

(7)

Last resting place of the rebels

Benburb Street, Dublin 7
heritageireland.ie
Luas, National Museum (Red Line); Dublin Buses 37, 38 and 39 stop nearby

Development space comes at a premium in Dublin's city centre, but one prime acre of land will never be built upon. Set between the former Collins Barracks and Ellis Quay, this quiet retreat is the last resting place of hundreds of rebels from the 1798 Rebellion.

The Croppies Acre is so-called for the Croppy Boys who fought in 1798. 'Croppy' refers to the closely cropped hairstyles worn by many of them – a style borrowed from French revolutionaries who cut their hair to distinguish themselves from wig-wearing aristocrats. After the Rebellion, up to 300 of those captured, hanged and beheaded were thrown into a mass grave – or Croppy Pit – on this land. (At the time, the area between Collins Barracks and the River Liffey would have consisted of marshy wasteland.) The Rebellion itself, mounted by United Irishmen against British Rule, saw tens of thousands of deaths and innumerable atrocities – the hairstyle that gave the Croppy Boys an identity also served to identify them for capture. A granite slab bearing the simple legend '1798' was erected by the Irish army in 1985, with the land officially opened as a memorial park on the bicentenary of the Rebellion in 1998.

The Croppies Acre was also the site of one of Dublin's best-known soup kitchens during the Famine. Established by the famous French chef, Alexis Soyer (appointed by the British government to dispense meals at a low cost to the Exchequer), the soup kitchen began operating in 1847 and within five months had served some 1 million meals, as Frank Hopkins writes in *Hidden Dublin: Deadbeats, Dossers and Decent Skins* (Mercier Press, 2007). Soup was dispensed from a 300-gallon (1,364-litre) boiler at the centre of a wooden building, with people admitted in lots signalled by the ringing of a bell. Renowned though Soyer was as a chef, however, there were complaints that his soup actually harmed some people suffering from dysentery …

ARTEFACTS IN STORAGE

Opening the archives

*National Museum of Ireland – Decorative Arts & History, Collins Barracks,
Benburb Street, Dublin 7
01 677-7444 – museum.ie
Tuesday, Wednesday, Friday and Saturday 10am–5pm, Thursday 10am–8pm,
Sunday and Monday 1pm–5pm
Closed Christmas Day, St. Stephen's Day and Good Friday
Admission: free
Luas, Museum (Red Line); Dublin Bus Stop 1475 is nearby on Wolfe Tone Quay*

For the first time in the history of Ireland's National Museum, artefacts kept in storage are accessible to everyone. Not all artefacts, of course – but enough to make you feel like a curator for an afternoon, thanks to the museum's hugely impressive 'visible storage' facility at Collins Barracks.

'What's in Store?' is an open-storage exhibition showcasing some of the museum's finest collections of glass, silver, pewter, brass, enamel and Asian applied arts. The Asian collections – including priceless lacquer, jade, ivory, statuary and metalwork – have not been on view since the museum opened at Collins Barracks in 1997. You can also see some of the ceramics collection, including 18th-century delftware, Belleek, Carrigaline and a brilliant collection of 18th- and 19th-century glass from Dublin, Cork, Belfast and Waterford. Much of the glass from the latter half of the 19th century is linked to the Pugh Glassworks, which produced a wide range of domestic and industrial glass from its Marlborough Street premises. Pugh brought a rare artistry and craft to its products, thanks to highly talented engravers like Franz Tieze and Joseph Eisert. In fact, no flint glass manufacture took place in Ireland from the closing of this facility in 1890 to the opening of Waterford Crystal (then Glass) in 1947.

Elsewhere, watch out for the row of Japanese samurai, ivories and enamels – including warrior armour dating from the Edo period (1600–1868). Exploring another aisle, you might stumble across archaeological glass, including Roman treasures from the second century BC. Or perhaps some vintage scientific instruments: watches, octants, sextants, telescopes and other devices from the 18th and 19th centuries, for instance. It's a whole other way of viewing a museum, and a brilliant complement to the more traditional displays.

ARBOUR HILL CEMETERY

A place of history and pilgrimage

Arbour Hill, Dublin 7
heritageireland.ie
Monday–Friday 8am–4pm, Saturday 11am–4pm, Sunday 9.30am–4pm
Dublin Bus stops 1713 and 1649 are a short walk away on Manor Street; routes
37 and 39 stop here, among others

Glasnevin is Dublin's best-known cemetery. Kilmainham Gaol is where many leaders of the 1916 Rising were executed. But this small green lung, set above the quays in Stoneybatter, is where 14 of the executed leaders were buried, 'while children played on the other side of the wall', as one note has it.

The first thing that strikes you about the place is how peaceful it is. Despite the tall, ominous walls of Arbour Hill Prison next door, the beautifully tended graves, mature trees and touches of TLC (a bird feeder here, a bowl of water for dogs there), make it feel welcoming. It jars with the events memorialised here. After the 1916 leaders were executed, their bodies were taken to Arbour Hill and covered with quicklime in an unmarked pit. In 1955, the prison parade ground, schoolyard and old cemetery here were amalgamated into a memorial park, and today the 'pit' is as smooth as a putting green, backed by a wall of Wicklow limestone on which the Irish Proclamation of Independence surrounds a gilded cross. The lettering took four years to be sculpted by Michael Biggs (you can also see his work on the commemorative tablet at the GPO, and the inscription on the Thomas Davis statue in Stephen's Green). A tricolour is mounted on a white flagpole alongside. A memorial ceremony is held at the cemetery each Easter.

Arbour Hill is also the last resting place of some 4,000 British military personnel and their families, who died while serving in Ireland from 1840 to 1876. If you examine the headstones stacked around the boundary walls, you can get a sense of their names, and where the soldiers served. Another secret portal, at the back of the cemetery, is a door leading through the wall to the Irish United Nations Veterans' Association (IUNVA) memorial garden. It is open from 10am to 2pm Monday to Friday, and from 10am to 12.30pm on Saturdays.

BURLAL CRYPTS

The mummies of St Michan's

St Michan's Church, Church Street, D7
01 872-4154 – facebook.com/stmichan
March–October: Monday–Friday 10am–12.30 pm and 2pm–4.30 pm, Saturday
10am–12.30pm; November–February: Monday–Friday 12.30pm–3.30pm,
Saturday 10am–12.30pm
Dublin Bus stops 1615 and 1616 are right outside St Michan's; Luas, Four
Courts (Red Line; 5-min walk)

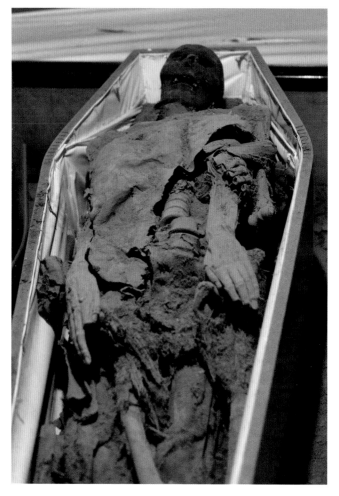

Fancy coming face to face with a 6ft 6in Crusader? That's just one of the experiences that awaits on a short but spooky tour of the crypts beneath St Michan's Church. The dry atmosphere in the limestone vaults here has caused dozens of bodies to mummify, and since Victorian times, visitors have descended through the padlocked iron doors in the graveyard to see them. Most famous of all is the Crusader, a frighteningly preserved specimen whose hands and fingers have been worn to a leathery shine by past visitors stroking them – a creepy connection that was said to bring good luck.

Dating from 1685, St Michan's is said to be the oldest parish church north of the River Liffey. Its exterior is dull and its interior plain though there are some fine wooden galleries and several items of interest, including an organ on which Handel is said to have practised before debuting his Messiah, and the original altar frontal from Dublin Castle's Chapel Royal – rescued from a market stall in the Liberties. But let's not kid ourselves: the main event is what lies beneath. 'Who wants to see the crypts?' as the blackly humorous guide says.

Visitors are led through stout iron doors into the netherworld, where myths and legends are detailed. Why is one body missing a hand and both of its feet, for example? And how old is the Crusader exactly? (On previous visits, Secret Dublin was told the mummy was 650 years old – a little young for the Crusades. On our latest tour, however, the age was put at 800 years). But there's plenty of verified history here too. One of the vaults contains the musty coffins of the Sheares brothers – hung, drawn and quartered for their role in the 1798 Rebellion. Another houses the Earls of Leitrim. All the coffins are ornately decorated save for one: that of the Third Earl, William Sydney Clements, a ruthless landlord who was assassinated in Milford, County Donegal, in 1878.

Sadly, St Michan's vaults fell victim to random desecration in 2019 when a man broke in, trashed several coffins and mummies, and made off with the Crusader's head. The macabre incident made news reports around the world – though thankfully, with the aid of CCTV, Gardaí identified the man within weeks and recovered the stolen skull. He was jailed for 28 months.

CHURCH STREET DISASTER MEMORIAL

A plaque, a street map of the area in 1913, brass fish and vegetables hanging from a lamppost …

Father Matthew Square, Church Street, Dublin 7
Dublin Bus stops 1615 and 1616 are nearby on Church Street; Luas, Four Courts (Red Line; 5-min walk)

On the evening of 2 September 1913, two tenement buildings on Church Street collapsed without warning. Several families lived in each of Nos 66 and 67, and the impact was disastrous, with seven residents losing their lives and others left maimed and injured in the rubble, according to contemporary newspaper reports. The youngest of the dead, Elizabeth Salmon, was just four and a half years old. Her brother Eugene (17) had rushed back into the building to try and save her, as their distraught father described in the *Evening Telegraph* the following day.

'Eugene took the youngest child (Josephine), aged one year and eight months, and brought her out safely. Then he went back for the other children, and got out with them alright, but it was when he was coming away with Elizabeth that they were struck by the falling masonry and killed.'

There's an intriguing memorial to the tragedy in today's Father Matthew Square — three elements you'd easily miss if you weren't looking for them. The first is a decorative lamppost — look up and you'll see brass fish and vegetables hanging from it just under the light, presumably a nod to the street stalls and Victorian fruit and vegetable markets nearby. Alongside is a plaque naming the dead, and a utility box painted with a street map of the area in 1913. Nos 66 and 67 are marked in red lettering … a touch that feels all the more powerful for its simplicity.

'It was a crisis or disaster waiting to happen,' Dr Jacinta Prunty, former head of the History Department at Maynooth College, says in a video featured on Century Ireland, a project compiled for Ireland's Decade of Centenaries 2012–2023. 'It could have been any of several hundred other houses in Dublin. It just happens to be those two.' The tragedy was a turning point, she explains, bringing the vexed issue of Dublin's slums to a reckoning. There was a public outcry, a huge attendance at the funerals, and relief funds and a Dublin Housing Inquiry were set up (the latter found that almost a quarter of families in Dublin at the time lived in one-room tenements).

'At this point, you couldn't just talk about it. You had to have action,' as Dr Prunty says. A new housing scheme was completed on Church and Beresford Streets by 1917, although this came too late for those remembered here.

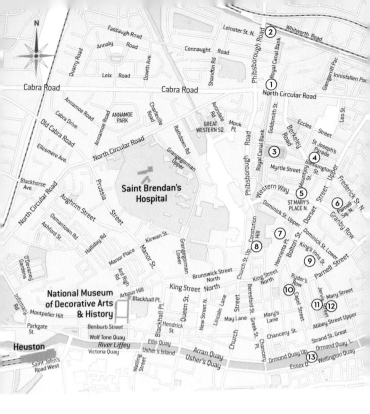

Centre North

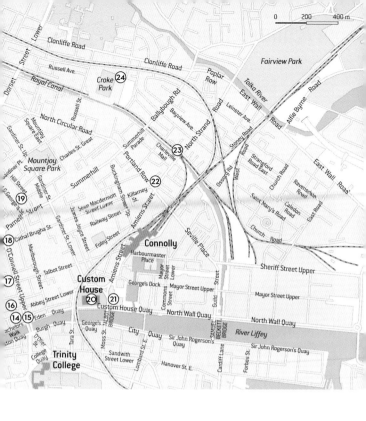

RIVERRUN GARDEN

The Dublin UNESCO City of Literature Garden

Phibsborough Library, Blacquiere Bridge, off North Circular Road, Dublin 7
01 830-4341
dublincity.ie
Monday–Wednesday 12.45pm–4pm & 4.45pm–8pm; Tuesday, Thursday,
Friday & Saturday 10am–1pm & 2pm–5pm; closed Sunday
The garden is visible beside the entrance gates at all times
Admission: free
Dublin Bus stops 81, 82 and 796 are nearby

James Joyce certainly got around Dublin City. And slowly but surely, memorials to the author are getting around it too. One of the most recent is the Dublin UNESCO City of Literature Garden, occupying a modest corner of Phibsborough Library's front lawn.

In spite of its grand title, the Riverrun Garden is still relatively unknown. It was designed to celebrate Dublin's being chosen as one of a handful of UNESCO World Cities of Literature in 2011 and was launched at that year's Bloom Festival in Phoenix Park. Bord Bia, the Irish Food Board, invited the City Council to exhibit, and the result, designed by the City Council's Parks & Landscape Services Division, went on to win two prizes – a Silver Medal and Best Overall Small Garden in Show. Poets like Gabriel Rosenstock and Anne Leahy read from their work here during Bloom, and after festivities wrapped at the Phoenix Park, the garden was transplanted to today's permanent location in Phibsborough.

On the face of it, Riverrun would appear to be a pretty straightforward celebration of Joyce's *Finnegans Wake*. Through the flowery space circles a miniature 'river' (when it's working), with various inscriptions linking the book's opening sentence and unfinished closing line: 'A way a lone a last a loved a long the riverrun, past Eve and Adam's, from swerve of shore to bend of bay, brings us by a commodius vicus of recirculation back to Howth Castle and Environs.' But there's more to it: the stones were salvaged from old city streets and buildings; the tree echoes the traditional gathering place for storytellers of yore, and a sculpture by Leo Higgins is reflected in the pool – as communities are reflected in the stories they tell.

In the words of its creators, 'The garden is symbolic of Dublin's ability to reinvent itself.'

NATIONAL FAMINE WAY

In the footsteps of the 1,490

Royal Canal, Phibsborough, Dublin 1
nationalfamineway.ie
Connolly DART station is a 5 to 10-min walk from the Royal Canal at
Newcomen Bridge; Dublin Bus stops 15 and 49 are on Dorset Street

In May of 1847, 1,490 people left Strokestown, County Roscommon to walk some 165 km to Dublin's docks. Black '47 was one of the worst years of the Famine (1845–1849), and the walkers were tenants of landlord Major Denis Mahon, who had offered them the grim choice of emigration (through 'assisted passage'), starvation on their blighted potato patch farms, or a place in the local workhouse. The 1,490, as they are still known, opted to emigrate, walking to join a packet steamer sailing from Dublin to Liverpool, and boats travelling onwards to Canada. Only half made it.

Famine memorials and interpretations exist all over the country – not least at the revamped National Famine Museum in Strokestown. But this 165-km trail, mostly following the emigrants' footsteps on off-road towpaths along the Royal Canal Greenway, is unique. 30 pairs of bronze children's shoes on plinths can be found along the route, and walkers or cyclists can also collect a 'passport' to fill with stamps along the way. Similar to the Camino de Santiago de Compostela, they can collect a certificate of completion at EPIC, The Irish Emigration Museum – this is where the route concludes, next to the Jeanie Johnston famine ship.

You can trace the Royal Canal through County Dublin, and spot the markers along the way – including a pair of bronze shoes near Croke Park. Some sections, particularly between the docks and Dorset Street, can feel forbidding, with litter strewn in and along the canal. Others, like the patch of post-industrial greenery between Dorset Street and Phibsborough Road (taking in Locks 3 and 4) is surprisingly pretty, with swans and herons in the reeds and locals sunning themselves in good weather. Watch out for the sculpture of Brendan Behan at Binn's Bridge – John Coll's artwork provides the author with a blackbird for company. The piece is engraved with the titles of Behan's works, including the Irish poem *Uaigneas* ('loneliness').

As for Major Denis Mahon, the landlord who prompted the tragic journey of the 1,490, he was assassinated in November 1847, after it emerged that so many of the tenants he sent away had died on their journey.

BLESSINGTON STREET BASIN

Dublin's Secret Garden

Blessington Street, Phibsborough, Dublin 7
01 830-0833 – 01 222-5278; dublincity.ie
Daylight hours
Admission: free
Connolly DART station (15–20-min. walk); Dublin Bus stops 189 and 196
(Phibsborough Road). The basin is a 10-min. walk from O'Connell Street

Looking for an off-radar park recommendation in Dublin? The Iveagh Gardens may be the stock tip, but this waterside oasis is the genuine hidden gem. Measuring just 0.75 hectares, the Blessington Street Basin is a short stroll from O'Connell Street, squirrelled away at the end of a beat-up street, yet almost totally unknown to Dubliners. Dating from 1810, when it opened with the aim of providing clean water to Dublin's northside, the park draws its supply from the Royal Canal. Though officially named 'the Royal George Reservoir' in honour of King George III, locals have always preferred 'the basin'. It no longer serves as a reservoir, however, offering a hush-hush little haven to visitors and local wildlife instead.

After walking past the gritty Georgian ghosts of Blessington Street, the trees, water and leafy central island come on like a bloom in spring –

with perimeter paths peppered with benches, Victorian-style lampposts, a fountain that spumes sporadically and the basin itself, bubbling with birdlife, waterfowl, butterflies, bats and fish. Sealed off by stone walls and circled by the terraces, chimneys and spires of Phibsborough, it's quite the surprise package.

Although capable of holding some 4 million gallons of water, it was only a matter of time before a burgeoning city required even more, and the Blessington Street Basin saw its function change after the introduction of the Vartry Reservoir in 1868. For the next century, its water went on to supply the Jameson and Powers' whiskey distilleries in the city, and it was formally opened as a public park in 1891. 'During the months when the roads are hard and dusty, and country walking is not always agreeable, a retreat, shaded, cool, and somewhat ornamented, must be appreciated,' noted a contemporary editorial in *The Irish Times*.

The present-day park layout is thanks to an inspired renovation in the early 1990s, when the fountain, railings and seating were added, and the manmade island bolstered to become a wildlife habitat. Watch out, too, for the park-keeper's lodge just inside the main entrance. Dating from 1811, its Tudor-style gables, colourful window boxes and pert chimneystacks are a perfect little pick-me-up after the dispiriting approach along Blessington Street.

Discs of history beneath our feet

Blessington Street, Phibsborough, Dublin 7
Connolly DART Station (15 to 20-min walk); Dublin Bus stops 189 and 196
(Phibsborough Road). Blessington Street is a 10-min walk from O'Connell
Street

Readers old enough to remember Dublin before September 1990 may recall rather smoggier city skies. That was the month the famous ban on the sale of bituminous or 'smoky' coal was introduced, in an effort to deal with the effect smog was having on the capital (and its residents' long-suffering lungs). According to some reports, the ban has resulted in air pollution levels falling by 70 percent.

Coal, of course, had been around for centuries by then. We often talk of the history beneath our feet, and on Georgian rows like Blessington Street, you only have to look down to see how embedded in everyday life it was. The dark, cast-iron discs beneath your feet are in fact covers for coal holes' – thin chutes through which tonnes and tonnes of black, dusty fossil fuel were funnelled into Georgian and Victorian homes. You'll notice more in the Merrion and Fitzwilliam areas of the city, or dotted beneath teetering strips like North Great George's Street and Henrietta Street. They're a visual link to a time when the city ran on the stuff, and coal stores lined its quays.

Coal hole covers are not uniform. Look closely, and you'll see an array of different designs, company names, features and ventilation holes cut into them – in some cases crisp and rigid; in others almost completely worn away by passing footsteps and use. Some of the designs are starkly geometric, while others are ornate, almost flowery. Some bear hypnotic circles or are surrounded by thin, carefully sculpted drainage channels. Designs were decorative, but also had the practical function of preventing people from slipping – you can also see the ghostly names of foundries like Sharkey or Tonge & Taggart. The covers measure several inches across; large enough to receive coal, but small enough to stop unwanted intruders from sneaking into cellars.

'It is amazing once you start to notice these old iron covers, how you almost cannot stop looking', as Arran Henderson of tour company Dublin Decoded writes in an engrossing, evocatively written blog post on his website, arranqhenderson.com. 'When a coal hole cover goes missing, is ripped out and filled in, it feels like a little piece of Dublin has died.'

ST MARY'S CHAPEL OF EASE ⑤

The Black Church

St Mary's Place, Broadstone, Dublin 7
Not officially open to visitors, as the building is occupied by several
businesses. Potential customers may be able to make an appointment,
however
Connolly Street DART station (20–25-min. walk); Dublin Bus stops 191 and
194, along the Western Way, are a short walk from St Mary's Place

Could this be the spookiest church in Dublin? Dating from 1830, the 'Black Church' got its nickname thanks to the calp limestone used in its construction – on wet days, it seems to take on a darkly ominous guise. The sense of foreboding is further ramped up by the hypodermic spires and slit-like windows of John Semple's Gothic Revival design. But that's not all. According to local lore, if you're brave (or foolish) enough to walk around St Mary's three times in an anti-clockwise direction at midnight, the devil will appear to steal your soul.

Austin Clarke, who grew up nearby, named a volume of his memoirs after St Mary's – its title, *Twice Round the Black Church*, falls just short of the circuits required to summon Old Nick. 'My childhood years were spent under the shadow of an edifice known locally as The Black Church,' the poet wrote. 'This Protestant Church on the north side of Dublin was grim and forbidding in appearance, and its popular name in the neighbourhood, with all its theological implications, was apt. Even before the age of reason, I was dimly aware of the *odium theologicum*, and when the sound of Sunday singing came faintly from the lancets behind the iron railing, I expected to see the devil loom terrifically from the leads.'

Similarly, in James Joyce's *Ulysses*, there is a moment when Leopold Bloom experiences the sins of the past (real or imagined) rising against him in a medley of voices, including 'a form of clandestine marriage with at least one woman in the shadow of the Black Church'.

St Mary's was deconsecrated in the 1960s, ostensibly because of the diminishing numbers at its services (a 'chapel of ease' is a secondary church in a parish, built for parishioners based further away from the principal place of worship). Today it's home to several businesses, and though not officially open to visitors, potential customers may be able to glimpse the interior by making an appointment with one of them. The most notable feature is Semple's extraordinary parabolic arch, a flowing design that seems to blur the distinctions between walls and ceiling, adding further to the Black Church's intrigue.

STAINED GLASS ROOM

The gallery within a gallery ...

Dublin City Gallery, The Hugh Lane, Parnell Square North, Dublin 1
01 222-5550
hughlane.ie
Tuesday–Thursday 10am–6pm; Friday & Saturday 10am–5pm; Sunday
11am–5pm; Closed Monday
Admission: free
Dart (Tara/Connolly Street; 15-min. walk). Luas: Abbey Street (10-min.
walk). Dublin Bus Stops 8, 10, 461 and 4726 are all nearby on Parnell Square

It's the Hugh Lane's gallery-within-a-gallery. To step into the Stained Glass Room in the Dublin City Gallery is to step momentarily into a whole other dimension – a whispery, church-like, and ridiculously beautiful room that twinkles like a heavenly disco ball.

The room is easy to miss if you're rushing towards more famous exhibits – Francis Bacon's cluttered studio, for example, or Jack B Yeats' stunning 'There is No Night'. But what's inside is unforgettable. The gallery's stained glass collection includes kaleidoscopic works by the likes of Harry Clarke, Evie Hone, James Scanlon, Wilhelmina Geddes and Paul Bony, backlit so gorgeously you could giggle. Stained glass has floated in and out of fashion in Irish arts circles over the years, but when you see a collection like this gathered together, when you can bask in its blooming colours, florid storytelling and intricate craftsmanship, the magic is plain to see.

The highlight is Harry Clarke's 'The Eve of St. Agnes'. Dating from 1924, this work consists of 22 small panels – each depicting a stanza of Keats's poem of the same title. The panels, split between two windows, tell the story of Madeline, a young heroine prevented from meeting her love because he is the sworn enemy of her family. According to an old superstition, however, virgin girls carrying out certain rituals on the eve of St. Agnes' feast day (January 20th) will see their loves come to them. So it transpires for Madeline, whom Clarke depicts in various panels lying 'lily-white' in her bed, watched over by her lover, and in scarcely disguised erotic union ('like a throbbing star … into her dream he melted…'), before their escape together into the storm. Phew!

To many, this is Clarke's (1889-1931) masterpiece, a beautiful and romantic work as sensual as the poem on which it is based. It's the highlight of a hidden room just crying out for a visit on a first date, Valentine's Day, or for anyone intending to get down on one knee…

More Harry Clarke windows can be seen in another unusual location – Bewley's Café on Grafton Street, where six magnificent examples were commissioned by Ernest Bewley and completed just prior to Clarke's death in 1931. You'll find them in the ground floor tearooms.

---

14 HENRIETTA STREET

Georgian Dublin's most fashionable address

Off Bolton Street, Dublin 1
14henriettastreet.ie
Wednesday–Sunday 10am–4pm; guided tours on the hour (visitors are
encouraged to book online); area walking tours also available
Tara Street or Connolly DART stations (20-min walk); Luas, Jervis (Red
Line; 10-min walk); Dublin Bus stops 8 and 10 are nearby on Granby Row

It's one of Dublin's great mysteries. How can its Georgian architecture be feted all over the world; how can its regal redbrick terraces and elegant set-piece squares be so celebrated in travel guides, while Henrietta Street is left to rot?

This, after all, is 'the single most intact and important architectural collection of individual houses – as a street – in the city', according to Dublin City Council's conservation plan. As an architectural site, the cobbled, early 18th-century street is 'as important to the record of settlement in these islands as ... Clonmacnoise or Wood Quay.' And yet, over time, Henrietta Street has fallen into disrepair, its crumbling houses only surviving thanks to the passion of a handful of residents and other committed parties. It's a short walk from O'Connell Street, but an effective cul-de-sac, a strip of decayed grandeur that feels like a Georgian galleon, adrift in an inner-city sea.

No.14 Henrietta Street brings a hit of hope. After a €4.5m refurbishment, this townhouse has opened as a superb small museum documenting the building's life as a mansion and subsequently a tenement. Guided tours begin by taking visitors back to its heyday when Henrietta Street (named after the Duchess of Grafton) was laid out between the 1720s and 1740s. For decades, it remained one of Dublin's most fashionable addresses, and No.14 was home to Lord Viscount Molesworth and his family.

Its next chapter was not so glamorous. After the Acts of Union, power shifted to London, and Dublin entered a period of economic decline. 14 Henrietta Street was occupied by lawyers, courts and even a barracks. By 1877, a landlord had torn out its grand staircase and carved it into 19 separate flats. By 1911, it was home to 100 people. The tour brings this period vividly to life, with recreated rooms and striking details like the 'Raddle Red' paint in the hallway, an overcoat stretched over a bed for warmth, or a preserved hand-written notice warning against tampering with 'anny ting' [sic].

Incorporating oral histories, memories and street songs, there's an absorbing social history journey behind this unassuming door, and the juxtaposition of cold, desperate tenements within the neoclassical spaces is startling. On Secret Dublin's visit, a guide even recounted the story of a man taking a horse to his flat. 'But one night the horse got the better of the floor, and went through onto the family underneath.'

THE HUNGRY TREE

An 'arboricultural curiosity'

Temple Gardens, King's Inns, Dublin 7
kingsinns.ie
treecouncil.ie
7am–7.30pm (or later)
Dublin Bus stops 1613, 1614 and 1619 are nearby on Constitution Hill. The
stops are served by the 83 and 83a routes between Kimmage and Harristown

Nature's revenge. The passage of time. Human folly. It's tempting to ascribe all manner of symbolic interpretations to this cartoonish phenomenon in Temple Gardens.

The Hungry Tree greets walkers, barristers and benchers as they enter the gardens at King's Inns from the south gate. It's a graphic spectacle: a hapless bench apparently being eaten alive by a London plane tree. The bench, like the others scattered about this handsome park, dates from the early 19th century. The plane's slow-motion gastronomic exploits have seen it listed as a heritage tree by the Tree Council of Ireland – alongside specimens like the 400-year-old mulberry at the Teacher Training College in Rathmines, reputed to be Dublin's oldest tree, and the Autograph Tree, a copper beech inscribed with the initials of visitors ranging from W. B. Yeats to George Bernard Shaw, in Coole Park, Co. Galway. Standing 21m high and measuring 3.5m in girth, the Hungry Tree is listed on the Heritage Tree Database as an 'arboricultural curiosity'. That senior members of an Inn of Court are known as 'benchers' only adds to its delight.

Inns of Court traditionally provided law students with accommodation, meals and tuition over the course of their studies. The King's Inns were designed by James Gandon and built in the early 1800s, although the Honorable Society of King's Inns (the governing body for barristers in Ireland) goes way back to the reign of Henry VIII – it was founded in 1541. Temple Gardens were opened to the public in the late 19th century, creating not only a welcome amenity for the working-class suburb in which they are set, but a handy short cut between Broadstone and Henrietta Street. The short cut is yet another surprise – an echoing, cobblestoned courtyard bookended by a triumphal arch added by architect Francis Johnson.

WILLIAMS & WOODS BUILDING

A hip hideaway in Dublin's first poured-concrete building

26 King's Inn Street, Dublin 1
chocolatefactory.ie
8am–4pm (café)
Admission: free entry to café customers
Luas, Jervis Street (Red Line), 5–10-min. walk

It's one of the most satisfying surprises in the inner city. There you are, strolling through an urban fudge of modern apartments, car parks and commercial developments when – bam! – a glorious maverick of a corner building comes into view. Williams & Woods was Dublin's first poured-concrete building, a former jam and marmalade factory run by a company that once supplied the city with its fix of Toblerone, Silvermints, 'Buttercup' toffees and the Irish Coffee Bar, among other brands.

It dates from 1910, with the original sign beautifully preserved on an angled corner … more than can be said for Williams & Woods' old HQ, an 18th-century hospital that was demolished after the company sold it in 1978 (a cinema occupies the site today).

Today, after years as a storage warehouse, the building has been given a new lease of life as the Chocolate Factory, a hive of studios housing photographers, designers, dancers, architects, up-cyclers, urban farmers and, at one stage, even a kung-fu academy.

It's an inspirational space, and the visitor may leave wondering why more of Dublin's neglected built heritage couldn't be rebooted in the same way. So many characterful old buildings with stories to tell are boarded up, sprouting weeds and falling into treacherous condition as politics, legal issues and plain old shenanigans play out.

Visitors can't tour the Chocolate Factory's studios, but everyone is welcome at the funky Blas Café situated in the wide-open, ground-floor space downstairs. Pared-back woods, big old iron-framed windows, lamps fashioned from cymbals and drums and a rolling gallery of artworks all serve as a setting for a loose and tasty menu (try the bacon and egg breakfast bap or the free-range chicken chipotle on sourdough). It's a hip space that will get you thinking about Dublin's social history all over again.

CAPEL PAWNBROKERS

Three brass balls …

108 Capel Street, Dublin 1
capelpawnbrokers.ie
Monday, Tuesday, Thursday and Friday 9am–5.30pm; Saturday 9am–7pm;
Closed Wednesday
Tara Street DART station (20-min walk); Luas, Jervis (Red Line; 5 to 10-min
walk); Dublin Bus stops 312 and 1479 are nearby on Ormond and Wellington
Quays

'The shop creaked with the weight of other people's sorrows.' So writes E. L. Wallant in his novel *The Pawnbroker* (HBJ, 1978). The quote is repeated in Jim Fitzpatrick's *Three Brass Balls: The Story of the Irish Pawnshop* (Collins Press, 2001) and the words will surely echo as you descend into the basement of No.108 Capel Street.

This is the address of Brereton's jewellery shop, but as the three vintage spheres suspended above its awning suggest, it's also one of Dublin's last remaining pawnshops. Golden spheres as a symbol of pawnbroking originated with the Medici family of Florence, whose bank was the largest in Europe in the 15th century. They also evoke the patron saint of pawnbrokers, Saint Nicholas of Myra, who legend says once helped a poor man with three daughters by throwing three golden purses into his house, thus providing the daughters with dowries. Don't expect to find Santa Claus in Capel Pawnbrokers, however. Just the fluorescent-edgy environment of a modern-day pawnshop, with security glass and sparse counters offset by a big old pledge book, some framed pawn tickets dating back to 1904, and of course, a window full of slightly sad-looking jewellery and trinkets – a golden bulldog with a bejewelled collar and a golden chain bearing the word 'Mum' were just two on Secret Dublin's visit.

There's been a pawnbroker on the site here since the 1850s. John Brereton took over the business in 1916, a time when Dublin was crawling with pawnbrokers, with as many as 50 'people's banks' surviving into the 1930s. Customers raised funds by selling everything from artificial limbs to their Sunday best ('for the pawnbroker, even the most ridiculous pledge would be accepted if he knew his customer', Fitzpatrick writes). Only three remain today, however – you'll also find brass balls hanging outside Carthy's of Marlborough Street and Kearns of Queen Street.

Capel Street was once a fashionable address, and even a short walk throws up all sorts of gems. Former Taoiseach Seán Lemass was born at No.2, there are some fine Georgian townhouses, and the Victorian shopfronts include John McNeill's (No.140) – today a pub, but formerly the music shop that made the bugle which sounded the Charge of the Light Brigade (1854). The street always seems to teeter between ruin and resurgence, but enjoyed a recent boost with new pedestrianisation measures.

HEADSTONES OF WOLFE TONE PARK

Headstones and the Hanging Judge …

Jervis Street, Dublin 1
Tara Street and Connolly DART stations (15-min walk); Luas, Jervis (Red Line); Dublin Bus stops 312 and 1479 are nearby on the quays

This small park, named after the Irish revolutionary Theobald Wolfe Tone (1763–1798), has a controversial history. Records show it was originally an 18th-century market space within the Jervis Estate, but went on to become the graveyard of St Mary's Church, where Wolfe Tone was baptised. Today, the church houses a bar and restaurant. Among those buried here was Lord Norbury, the famous 'Hanging Judge' of 1798, who counted Robert Emmet among those he sent to the gallows. After his death in 1831, Norbury is said to have haunted Dublin's streets as a black dog.

Something else that haunted the city, in Georgian times and after, was its stomach-churning sanitation and overcrowding. When the Reverend James Whitelaw was compiling his census from 1798–1805, he noted that St Mary's parish contained 'about 16,654 souls' and its churchyard 'about 32,000 square feet. Hence the proportion for each inhabitant is not two square feet, and it is a fact, which I have witnessed, that in order to make room for others, bodies in that cemetery have been taken up in an absolute state of putrefaction, to the great and very dangerous annoyance of the vicinity.'

Thankfully the situation had improved long before the church was deconsecrated in 1966. After that, its graveyard was transformed into a traditional 'garden park' layout, with headstones stacked against the wall. Dublin City Council oversaw its redesign in 2001, and according to *Excavations.ie,* the database of Irish excavations reports, '11 museum boxes of human skeletal material' were uncovered. However, the new urban plaza paved over most of the greenery, with some headstones set into the ground around the perimeter, and became not only a social space, but often an anti-social one, with headstones often walked on or even driven over. A local community campaign (wolftonepark.com) agitated for its return to a garden-style layout, and the Council itself has since admitted that events held there 'in hindsight were probably not appropriate in a former burial ground.'

The park's latest iteration came in 2022, with new works comprised of a fresh lawn, trees and plants, creating what the Council describes 'as an oasis of green space'. Visitors can make their own mind up about whether it succeeds, but at least the headstones have been surveyed and inventoried by the City Archaeologist, hence their numbering. Just keep your eye out for a suspicious looking black dog …

RENATUS HARRIS ORGAN

Where Dublin's history meets modern DJs

The Church, Jervis Street, Dublin 1
thechurch.ie
Bar from 10.30am; gallery from 5pm
Tara Street and Connolly DART stations (15-min walk); Luas, Jervis (Red Line); Dublin Bus stops 312 and 1479 are nearby on the quays

Most visitors to The Church, it's probably fair to say, are expecting DJs and live traditional music rather than a Renatus Harris organ once played by George Frederick Handel. But this beautifully restored instrument isn't the only surprising feature among the interiors of this well-known pub and restaurant in the former St Mary's Church on Jervis Street.

In its former life, the superpub was a Protestant church. Dating from 1702, the building took its name from a medieval monastery that once sprawled north of the River Liffey and seems to have predominantly been the work of William Robinson, the architect responsible for Kilmainham's Royal Hospital. St Mary's was the first church in Dublin to boast a gallery, and that feature remains in place today, with restaurant tables overlooking a long bar at ground level, and the early 18th-century organ that is the building's centrepiece. A couple of chipped keys aside, the instrument is largely unaltered since it was played by Handel, who debuted his Messiah in Dublin and lived for a time on nearby Abbey Street. It was designed by the master English organ-maker Renatus Harris (1652–1724), and today, its golden pipes form an extraordinary backdrop to one of the biggest drinking spaces in the city. In fact, diners can sit right up beside the ivory keys and stop knobs once tinkled upon by Handel himself ('it is known that he regularly used the organ here to practise', as today's website states).

The church, which was refurbished in the 2000s, contains several other artefacts. There's a bust of Arthur Guinness to celebrate his marriage here in 1761. A stained glass window is framed with Portland stone. A baptismal font may have captured water from the brows of Seán O'Casey and Wolfe Tone, who were among 25,000 souls christened at St Mary's. The Cellar Bar, a cocktail bar and events space, now haunts the former crypts, and wooden floorboards leading from the gallery into a glass-enclosed tower connected to the building were rescued from the Adelphi Cinema. Prior to its demolition in 1995, the Adelphi had hosted performances from The Beatles, Johnny Cash and Roy Orbison, among countless other legends. Their names are listed here.

HIPPOCAMPUS LAMPS

Henry Grattan's Hippocampi

Grattan Bridge,
Dublin 2
Tara Street DART station (15-min. walk); Luas, Jervis Street (Red Line;
5–10 min. walk); Dublin Bus stops 312 and 1479 are nearby on the quays

Dubliners widely refer to it as Capel Street Bridge, but the stone and cast-iron structure straddling the Liffey between Capel Street and Parliament Street is in fact named after Henry Grattan (1746–1820). It dates from the 1870s, when its precursor was adapted to include cast-iron supports, footpaths on either side of the road and ornate street furniture – including several of the city's most intriguing cast-iron lamp standards.

The pale green lamps, set at intervals along the railings, are each propped up by a pair of curvy seahorses – or more correctly, Hippocampi. Bearing the head and forequarters of a horse and the tail of a fish, these powerful creatures are best known from Greek and Roman mythology, where they pull Poseidon and Neptune's sea-chariots. However, 'Capel' is also pleasingly similar to the Irish word for horse (*capall*), and water horses also feature in Celtic mythology, where shape-shifting beasts like the *each-uisce* and Kelpie are described as luring humans to their deaths in the lakes and streams they haunt.

Evocative as the cast-iron Hippocampi are, however, they're much more likely to be simple symbols of Dublin's status as a maritime port. For much of the 18th century, Capel Street (actually named for Arthur Capel, the First Earl of Essex) was the city's primary thoroughfare and one of its most fashionable addresses. At that time, the Custom House was located on Essex Quay at the site of the present-day Clarence Hotel, and hard as it is to imagine today, the area would have run thick with ships and sails. Several features of the bridge have come and gone over the years – from a statue of George I on horseback to Continental-style kiosks erected in the noughties – but the Hippocampi have survived.

Two similar cast-iron Hippocampi can be found flanking the statue of Henry Grattan on College Green. Sculpted by John Henry Foley and erected in 1874, the statue was originally surrounded by four such lamps, but they were removed several decades ago.

Put that in your pipe and smoke it

34a Bachelors Walk,
Dublin 2
Luas Green and Red Lines stop at nearby O'Connell Street and Abbey Street;
Tara Street DART station is nearby; and dozens of bus routes pass through the
area

Dublin has its ghosts. Thankfully, for those of us enthralled by the depths and textures of the city's urban fabric, it also has its ghost signs. Think of the black and orange 'Bolands Flour Mills' lettering overlooking Grand Canal Dock – somehow surviving as office towers sprout all around. Consider those mysterious doorway mosaics, or the Finn's Hotel sign on Leinster Street South (see p. 154). These little clues, whether left by accident or design, are reminders of the richness of Dublin's shifting streetscape, of the businesses, trends and characters that have come and gone in a city that seems at once stubbornly similar and ever-changing.

Look closely at the small blue shopfront at No. 34a Bachelors Walk and you'll see another clue. There, beneath contemporary signs for the Dublin Cultural Institute, next to Starbucks, a pair of older wooden plaques bears the protruding letters 'KP'. What do they mean? Where have they come from?

KP refers to Kapp & Peterson. Older Dubliners will recall the famous pipemakers, a dyed-in-the-wool Victorian brand that once seemed part of the city furniture. Its origins lay with German brothers George and Frederick Kapp, who established a pipe-making business in London in 1865. Shortly afterwards, Frederick struck out on his own with a shop on Grafton Street, where he teamed up with Charles Peterson, a young Latvian. Charles was the master craftsman responsible for several of the company's patented designs, and it is his name that survives today – there is a Peterson pipe shop at No. 48–49 Nassau Street (Charles 'turned a pipe dream into a dream pipe', as a promotional video on its website puts it).

Kapp & Peterson first took possession of the Bachelors Walk shop after the 1916 Rising: in a contemporary newspaper clipping posted on Petersons' Pipedia page (pipedia.org/wiki/Peterson), the building is referred to as 'one of the most shot-at and bullet-punctured premises in Dublin'. Look up from the O'Connell Street side, and you can also see a much larger Kapp & Peterson painted sign on the corner building's rooftop. Until recently, another of these signs was visible from O'Connell Bridge and the south quays … though this now seems to have faded or been removed.

Perhaps that's the nature of ghost signs. Rarely protected, often vulnerable to the whims of businesses, fashion or time, you never know where they'll crop up … or disappear. In Dublin, Instagram site @dublinghostsigns is a great starting point for locating those that survive.

BULLET HOLES IN THE O'CONNELL MONUMENT

A legacy of the 1916 Rebellion …

O'Connell Street, Dublin 1
Dart (Tara Street or Connolly Street DART stations); Luas, Abbey Street
(Red Line); Dublin Bus; Dublin Bus stops 271, 273 and others are nearby on
O'Connell Street

Pigeon droppings and the passage of time aren't the only things to have taken their toll on the O'Connell Monument. Look closely at the statue of Daniel O'Connell on his granite plinth, at the bronze figures swarming about in the frieze below, at the four winged victories above the base. They're peppered with dozens of small holes, drilled by whizzing bullets.

The bullet holes are a legacy of the 1916 Rebellion and the turbulence that followed, including the Irish War of Independence and the Civil War that erupted after the establishment of the Free State in 1922. Clearly, the intersection of O'Connell Street and the city quays hasn't just been a busy junction for traffic. During the course of recent restoration works, no fewer than 10 bullet holes were identified in the 12m-high figure of O'Connell alone, two of which pierced his head. In total, there are approximately 30 bullet holes in the monument.

Daniel O'Connell was one of Ireland's towering historical figures. Following his death in 1847, the committee responsible for the monument resolved that it should memorialise 'O'Connell in his whole character and career, from the cradle to the grave, so as to embrace the whole nation'. Though a fund was established soon after his funeral, it wasn't until 1882 that the result – to a design by John Henry Foley – was officially unveiled: O'Connell tops the plinth, with four winged victories representing patriotism, courage, eloquence and fidelity at the bottom. Sandwiched between the two is a frieze of some 30 figures, including the Maid of Erin, her breast punctured by perhaps the most visible of the bullet strikes.

What would the Great Emancipator have felt about his statue being showered in a hail of gunfire? In truth, O'Connell was no stranger to weaponry. In 1815 he was even challenged to a duel by John D'Esterre, a member of Dublin Corporation, which ended with D'Esterre being mortally wounded by a shot to the hip. Tradition holds that the memory haunted O'Connell for the rest of his life – so much so that he wore a black glove on his right hand when receiving Holy Communion.

It's not only Dublin's grandest monument that bears O'Connell's name, of course. O'Connell Street itself is Dublin's widest boulevard, and bullet holes are only the start of its secrets.

INDEUPENDENT HOUSE CLOCK   ⑯

Serving time on Middle Abbey Street

Independent House
Middle Abbey Street, Dublin 1
Tara Street and Connolly DART stations (5 to 10-min walk); Luas, Abbey
Street (Red Line); Dublin Bus stops 271, 310 and 4496 are nearby on
O'Connell Street

Although today's postal address finds the *Irish Independent* on Talbot Street, the building historically associated with the newspaper is Independent House.

Dating from 1924, this was the headquarters of the *Irish Independent*, *Evening Herald* and *Sunday Independent* for almost 80 years before the group relocated. It was sold in 2003, and at one point was earmarked to become part of a 'Northern Quarter' retail district, according to a report in *The Irish Times*. Like so many other Celtic Tiger plans, however, it fell foul of the recession. Today, Independent House is owned by retail group Primark, but sadly, despite the relatively well-maintained exterior, remains vacant.

Although the newspapers and their staff have decamped to Talbot Street (the publications are today owned by Mediahuis Ireland, part of the European media group based in Belgium), several nostalgic traces remain. The newspaper titles can still be seen on the building's façade, for example. Until recently, little hooded letterboxes once used for correspondence, classified ads and competitions were at street level – a throwback to an era of snail mail rather than social media. Look up, and you'll also see a copper-framed clock protruding from the middle of four recessed columns, connected to the third storey by a precarious-looking access bridge. Eagle-eyed observers (or those with binoculars) can see the words 'Stokes Cork' – the company that made it. The clock is stopped nowadays, but it's an atmospheric throwback to a time before everybody had phones, or indeed watches. Other famous Dublin clocks include those at Pen Corner on Dame Street, the Happy Ring House on O'Connell Street, and of course, the *Irish Times* clock – which, unlike the Independent House one, moved with that newspaper from its historic location on D'Olier Street to its current address on Tara Street.

The Irish Independent wasn't the first newspaper run from Middle Abbey Street. This block had previously been home to *The Nation*, a nationalist newspaper founded by Thomas Davis, Charles Gavan Duffy and John Blake Dillon in 1842, as a bronze plaque outside the same building recalls. What will become of Independent House and its clock remains to be seen, although it is a protected structure.

GPO MUSEUM & COURTYARD

(17)

The spiritual heart of Dublin

GPO, O'Connell Street, Dublin 1
01 872-1916
anpost.com/Witness-history
Tuesday–Saturday 10am–5pm
Closed on public holidays (but not Bank Holidays); Guided tours available
DART (Tara Street or Connolly station, 10-min. walk); Luas (Red Line,
Abbey Street, 2-min. walk); Dublin Bus stops 4496 and 6059 are nearby on
O'Connell Street

Every Dubliner knows the GPO's iconic façade. It was here, on 24 April 1916, that Padraig Pearse read the Proclamation of the Irish Republic. The building's columns and Portland stone portico were the only parts of the General Post Office still standing after the Easter Rising and naturally, 100 years later, it played a central role in the Irish state's centenary commemorations.

But the GPO's central courtyard? That's not so familiar. To access this space, visitors need to buy a ticket for one of the city's newer 'visitor experiences', GPO Witness History. It's worth the outlay.

Passing into the historic building's basement, interactive displays quickly immerse you in the stories of this controversial rebellion – from its social and political context to its momentous aftermath, from big names to the small moments (personal artefacts include Éamonn Ceannt's razor and Countess Markievicz's leather-bound prayer book). A 15-minute audiovisual experience brings to life the circumstances that led to the Rising, including the cultural revival and struggle for Home Rule. There are lots of touchscreens and video booths too.

The courtyard comes as the visitor journey ascends back to ground level. Beautifully remodelled ahead of the 2016 commemorations, its brickwork is crisp, its vaulted and sash windows intricate, its rooftops seeming almost to be pierced by the spire, which soars 120m above O'Connell Street outside.

It's easy to imagine the horses and mail carts that would have passed through the yard in bygone times, and a nicely understated art installation by Barbara Knezevic features 40 shards of rock mirrored on stainless steel. *They Are of Us All* remembers the 40 children killed during the Easter Rising. For a fleeting moment, standing dead centre in such a symbolic space, it feels like you're at the spiritual heart of the city.

Afterwards, of course, you exit through a gift shop. What the 1916 leaders would have thought of the t-shirts, key-rings and tea towels commemorating their struggle we will never know, but the bright and cheerful café is a bonus. Grab a coffee overlooking the courtyard, while the crowds pile up and down O'Connell Street oblivious to its very existence.

THE CAB DRIVERS' SHRINE

Erected by ordinary Dubliners

Cathal Bruga Street, Dublin 2
Luas, Abbey Street (Red Line; 5-min. walk) or O'Connell Street (Green Line; 5-min. walk); Tara Street or Connolly DART stations (5–10-min. walk); Dublin Buses 4496 and 6059

The taxi drivers at the northern end of O'Connell Street have been as much a fixture of Dublin's main boulevard as the GPO or the O'Connell Monument. Walk past day or night, and you'll find a cabal of cabbies lining up opposite the Savoy Cinema – sharing gossip, sucking on cigarettes, reading papers or honking horns to move the line along.

Just as much a fixture, though less noticed, is the statue of Jesus that, until recently, sat at the head of the rank. (Following Luas works, it is now located close by on Cathal Brugha Street.) Standing on a granite plinth, encased in a PVC box, Christ is depicted with arms outstretched and Sacred Heart blooming like a flower in the centre of His chest. He stands on a rock painted with stars – look closely, and you'll not only see spots of blood in His palms, but toenails painted a pale peach.

Despite its modern casing, the Christ figure has been here since the Civil War, when horse-drawn cab drivers helped to rescue goods and furniture from shops set ablaze on O'Connell Street. The salvaged goods were left in the centre of the street for shop-owners to reclaim them, the story goes, but nobody came for the Sacred Heart. The cabbies duly got some boxes from Moore Street and set it up as a temporary shrine. To this day, it remains the only memento of fighting on O'Connell Street.

'May God bless the taxi driver's [sic], keep them safe and watch over them on there journey's [sic],' the current plaque reads. 'In Memory of Eugene Lawlor, Rank Organiser, RIP.'

Its colours and its grammar have made the shrine the subject of some pretty snarky comments over the years. While it's true that it won't end up in the Saatchi Gallery, the more you look at it, the more touching it becomes. The grammar is so obviously atrocious, it seems to underline the endearing honesty of it all. There's no poetry or pretence, and Christ Himself is modest, in contrast to the bronze depictions of O'Connell, Parnell and others nearby – not to mention the 120m Dublin Spire.

'For ages I thought this was some poncey modern art exhibit,' as one passer-by posted on Yelp. 'Then I got a closer look at it. It's actually quite a touching memorial … it's also nice to know that a community, like the taxi drivers, can have their values represented right in the heart of the city.'

NO. 7 ECCLES STREET FRONT DOOR

The most famous door in Irish fiction …

James Joyce Centre, 35 North Great George's Street, Dublin 1
01 878-8547; jamesjoyce.ie
Tuesday–Saturday 10am–5pm, Sunday 12 noon–5pm
Tara Street and Connolly DART stations (10-min. walk); Dublin Buses 120,
4, 40b, 40d, 7, 7d and 8 stop at bus stop 4725 on nearby O'Connell Street

Step through the front door of 35 North Great George's Street, and you'll find a local literary treasure: the James Joyce Centre. But there's a more interesting front door in the backyard.

No. 7 Eccles Street was the fictional home of Leopold Bloom, the central character in James Joyce's *Ulysses*. Although Joyce himself only stayed at the address for one night in 1909, it is central to his novel. It is here that we meet Bloom as he prepares breakfast in bed for his wife, Molly. It is from here that he leaves on his peregrinations around the city, and to here that he returns in the wee hours, famously forgetting his front-door key.

'Why was he doubly irritated?'

'Because he had forgotten and because he remembered that he had reminded himself twice not to forget.'

In 1909 Joyce had watched as his friend John Francis Byrne, who lived at No. 7, similarly climbed over the front railings having forgotten his latch key. The events of that day obviously made an impression: Byrne and Bloom share the same height and weight.

Today, the front door to No. 7 is kept under an awning. It's an underwhelming setting, to say the least, but at least it is a setting. In the 1960s, the Georgian terrace incorporating No. 7 Eccles Street was razed to facilitate the expanding Mater Private Hospital. The door was only rescued thanks to the intervention of Patrick Kavanagh, Flann O'Brien and John Francis Ryan, owner of The Bailey pub. By all accounts, their negotiations to buy the door almost collapsed after the nuns who owned the land learned of its connection with 'that pagan writer', but the transaction went ahead, and the door was taken to The Bailey, where it remained until its donation to the James Joyce Centre.

Today, reunited with its stone frame, the portal to No. 7 looks strangely distressed. The knocker and handles are rusty, the paint chipped, the wood cracking in places – hardly befitting the most famous front door in Irish fiction. But it's as moving a memorial to 'the mummy and the daddy' of Irish writers, as Frank McGuinness dubs Joyce in a video upstairs, as you'll find in his native city.

JAMES GANDON'S DESK

Where Dublin landmarks were designed

Custom House Visitor Centre, Custom House Quay, Dublin 1
heritageireland.ie
Daily 10am–5.30pm
Connolly and Tara Street DART stations are less than five minutes' walk
away; Dublin Bus stop 407 is right outside

'This is James Gandon's original desk. He would have sat here to draw up plans of the Custom House.'

That's the simple descriptive note set on a modest desk inside the revamped Custom House Visitor Centre. Gandon (1742–1823) was the English-born architect responsible for several of Dublin's iconic buildings – the Four Courts, King's Inns, O'Connell Bridge (then Carlisle Bridge) and Custom House among them. This visitor centre tells the story

of Dublin from the late 1700s and of the neoclassical building itself – arguably the greatest challenge tackled on that small desk.

The Custom House was designed to alleviate shipping logjams further up the Liffey. Previously, Dublin's 'city centre' lay upriver near Grattan Bridge, which links Capel and Parliament Streets. At the time, this was the last bridge before the Irish Sea, with the old Custom House set on the river alongside it. Gandon's new building faced numerous challenges – it was to be built on swampy ground, and was fiercely opposed by the merchant classes, fearful of shifting the axis of the city. 'While the foundations were being dug, a comet appeared in the sky over Dublin', one display says. 'It was visible at night for almost two weeks, and many saw it as a bad omen.'

Despite all of this, the building was complete by 1791 – with details including river gods carved into the façade by Edward Smyth, a sculptor Gandon described as 'equal to Michelangelo'. The achievements of Gandon himself, who had been forced to keep a low profile when he first arrived (and who left Ireland for a time during the 1798 Rebellion) also came to be valued as time went on. An inscription on his grave in Drumcondra reads: 'Such was the respect in which Gandon was held by his neighbours and friends from around his home in Lucan, that they refused carriages and walked the 16 miles to and from Drumcondra on the day of his funeral.'

130 years after the Custom House was completed came an event you might say was portended by that comet. In 1921, IRA volunteers set the building ablaze in a key action of the War of Independence (the Custom House was viewed as 'the administrative heart of the British civil service machine', as Republican Oscar Traynor put it). It was a propaganda win, but it also left nine dead, destroyed the building and its records, and saw many volunteers captured. Restored by 1930, today it houses the Department of Housing, Local Government and Heritage.

FREE FLOW ㉑

A surreptitious movement towards the sea …

North Wall Quay, Dublin Docklands
Tara Street DART station (10-min. walk); Luas, George's Dock (Red Line;
5–10-min. walk); Dublin Bus stops 6252 and 2499 are nearby at Sean
O'Casey Bridge

Dublin's Docklands aren't the first place you'd associate with art in the city. Nevertheless, there's a surprising collection of public commissions lining the quays in the area. A bronze linesman hauls a rope on City Quay. Reflective sequins mask a Bord Gáis installation near The 3Arena, recalling the banded wrapping of the freight containers once common on the River Liffey. Rowan Gillespie's *Famine* haunts Custom House Quay.

Most surprising of all is Rachel Joynt's *Free Flow* (2005), an installation of hundreds of small, internally lit glass cobbles set along a section of the north quays stretching from the Custom House to North Wall. Joynt's other public works in Dublin include *People's Island* (1988), a collection of footprints and birds' feet set in bronze in a busy traffic island on O'Connell Bridge, and *Arc Hive* (2003), a series of honeycomb-like grids inlaid into the floor of Pearse Street Library. *Free Flow* conveys the same sense of discovery and detail; it's a sculpture stumbled upon underfoot, coaxing passers-by to engage first with the pavement, then with the place. Peppered along North Wall Quay, the light fixtures hide away hundreds of silver and copper fish, suspended within stainless steel halos. The lights themselves are watery shades of green and blue, helping to suggest 'an almost surreptitious movement towards the sea', as the artist puts it. They recall *Starboard* (2001), Joynt's translucent ship plan on Gregg's Quay in Belfast, as well as *Mothership* (1999), her cast bronze sea urchin at Sandycove.

The sense of discovery in her public art 'is paramount', Joynt has said. 'I don't want a sign telling people what to do,' as she explained in a piece in the *Irish Arts Review*. And that's exactly what makes *Free Flow* such a stumbled-upon delight.

22

THE FIVE LAMPS

Hang yer bollix off it!

Junction of Portland Row & Strand Street, Dublin
*Connolly DART station (5-min. walk); Luas, Connolly (Red Line; 5-min.
walk); Dublin Bus stops 516 and 619 are nearby*

A t first glance, there appears to be little doubt as to how the Five Lamps got its name. The landmark stands at a busy junction in the north inner-city, with the five lamps sprouting from its cast-iron column echoing the five streets – Portland Row, North Strand Road, Seville Place, Amiens Street and Killarney Street – that intersect around it.

It's a key reference point for directions in the area. 'Carry on past the Five Lamps,' someone might say. Or 'It's not far from the Five Lamps.' Friends, sporting teams, walking groups and countless others have used the landmark as a rendezvous point; there's been a city arts festival and brewery named after it and it's said that no-one born north of the Five Lamps can really call themselves a true Dubliner. Others delight in pointing out the black-and-gold standard, before delivering one of the city's greatest quips: 'Hang yer bollix off it.'

The Five Lamps refer to more than the five-point junction, however. Dating from the late 1800s, they were originally erected as a memorial to General Henry Hall, a celebrated veteran of the British Army's campaigns in India. As Christine Casey writes in *Dublin* (Yale University Press, 2005), Hall is said to have 'raised a corps among a wild race of Imhairs, whom he civilised by inducing them to abandon their habits of murder and infanticide.' Afterwards, he settled in Galway, and the monument is said to commemorate five key battles fought on the subcontinent. The Five Lamps survived the fallout from another great battle in 1941, when German aircraft bombed Dublin's North Strand – a small memorial park to the 28 people killed and 90 injured on that fateful occasion, together with a colourful wall mural, can be found nearby on Amiens Street.

As you get closer to the lamppost, look out for four lions' heads on its column. These survive from a time when the original gas-lit fixture incorporated a fountain. Water spurted from the lions' mouths into four basins at its base, drinking cups were chained to the structure, and both humans and horses would have enjoyed a passing sup. Sadly, though the elegant lamp standard survives, it seems rather at sea today amid an ugly jumble of CCTV poles, traffic lights and street signage, not to mention the mélange of derelict buildings and charmless modern apartment and commercial blocks surrounding it.

ROYAL CANAL AND LOCKKEEPER'S COTTAGE

23

The Auld Triangle went jingle jangle …

Newcomen Bridge, North Strand Road, Dublin 1
Connolly DART station (10 to 15-min walk); Luas, Connolly (Red Line; 10 to 15-min walk); Dublin Bus stops 516 and 618 are on North Strand Road

Once upon a time, canals were the motorways of Ireland. In their heyday, tens of thousands of passengers and hundreds of thousands of tonnes of freight were carried by horse-drawn barges along the Royal Canal and Grand Canal every year. Over time, of course, railways and roads went on to replace these watery thoroughfares, and today their fates are mixed. In Dublin, the Grand Canal is an idyllic vision of greenery, sculptures and cycle paths as it approaches the Liffey, but the Royal Canal can feel like the forgotten child. Since its closure, restoration has been slow.

The Royal Canal dates from 1789, although poor surveying meant it didn't reach the River Shannon until 27 years (and 47 locks) later. Its outlet at the River Liffey can be seen at Spencer Dock, built by the Midland Great Western Railway Company, but there's another fascinating piece of built heritage at the first lock. Just beneath Newcomen Bridge on the North Strand Road, a few metres from the hulking Croke Park, sits a two-room lockkeeper's cottage dating from the 1790s. Not too long ago, a family had rented the cottage and there was pride in its upkeep – smart white paint, splashy flowers and wooden shutters delighted passers-by. When Secret Dublin stopped by recently, it was unoccupied, with Waterways Ireland considering options for its future use. However, if you block out the surrounding clutter of billboards, railway lines and flats, the scene looks very similar to how it might have done over 200 years ago – when keepers living in the cottage tended the gates, beams and chamber of the double lock.

From Newcomen Bridge, it's possible to follow the canal west towards Ashtown. Scenery along the route ranges from leafy to bleak and unforgiving – most notably as it passes the walls of Mountjoy Prison. This is where Brendan Behan famously set his 'Auld Triangle', going 'jingle jangle / All along the banks of the Royal Canal'. Walking beneath the stands of Croke Park, imagine the rousing rendition performed by Bono and The Edge during U2's 360° Tour, when they dedicated the ballad to perhaps its finest interpreter – Ronnie Drew of The Dubliners.

MURDER AND THE GAA MUSEUM

From a hurling murder to Muhammad Ali's shorts

Croke Park Stadium, Cusack Stand entrance (off St Joseph's Ave.)
01 819-2323
crokepark.ie
Monday–Saturday 9.30am–5pm, Sunday 10am–5pm
Connolly DART station (15–20-min. walk); Dublin Bus stops 499 and 500
are nearby on Summerhill Parade

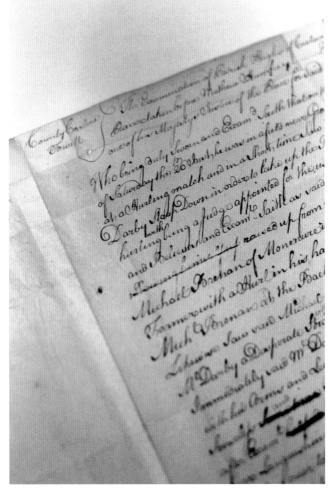

t's surprising that more people aren't killed playing hurling. Think about it … 30 sinewy athletes battling against each other with axe-shaped sticks and a sliotar (hard leather ball) belted about at speeds of up to 180kmph.

'It looks like there's a bit of a shemozzle in the parallelogram,' as commentator Micheál Ó hEithir once quipped … although it mostly stops short of murder.

Mostly. Croke Park is Ireland's 82,300-capacity sporting cathedral, and though inter-county games are highlights, there's a lot more to it than live action. A brilliant suite of stadium and rooftop tours rivals those at the Nou Camp or Old Trafford, and buried deep beneath the Cusack Stand you'll find a GAA Museum that really should be better known. Displays range from historical artefacts (check out Michael Cusack's blackthorn stick, or the ref's whistle from the Bloody Sunday massacre of 1920) to famous kits and medals; from halls-of-fame and interactive sporting challenges to the Liam McCarthy and Sam Maguire cups themselves. Croke Park has been known to host other sports too, as Muhammad Ali's shorts and gloves from a 1972 bout with Al 'Blue' Lewis attest.

Amidst all of this is displayed a yellowing document, a handwritten witness statement describing a trial in 1785. It recounts the actions of one Michael Brennan during a hurling match in Co. Laois that year. Brennan 'came behind the back of Patrick McDarby and with the flatt of his hurl … he gave a desperate stroak of same on the head,' the statement reads. 'McDarby fell upon his face upon the Ground with his armes and legs extended … in a few minutes some people came up and turned [him onto] his back and then he was immediately blooded and heard several people then say he was killed and would never recover.' Thankfully, today's athletes wear helmets.

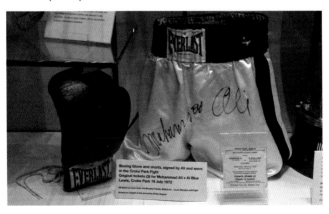

Boxing Glove and shorts, signed by Ali and worn in the Croke Park Fight
Original tickets (3) for Muhammad Ali v Al Blue Lewis, Croke Park 19 July 1972

Centre South

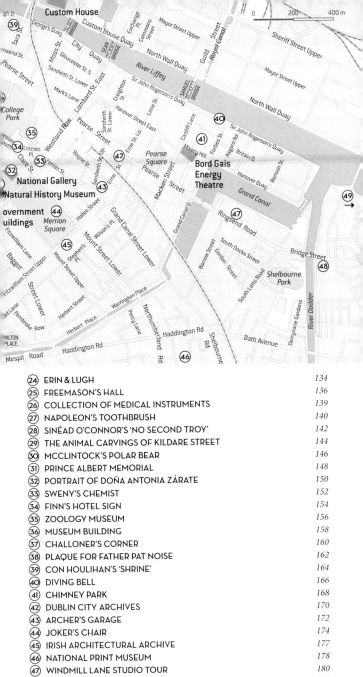

ISOLDE'S TOWER

The hidden heart of Dublin's medieval defences

Exchange Street Lower, Dublin 8
Tara Street DART station (5–10-min. walk); Dublin Bus stop
1443; Luas, Jervis Street (Red Line; 5–10-min. walk)

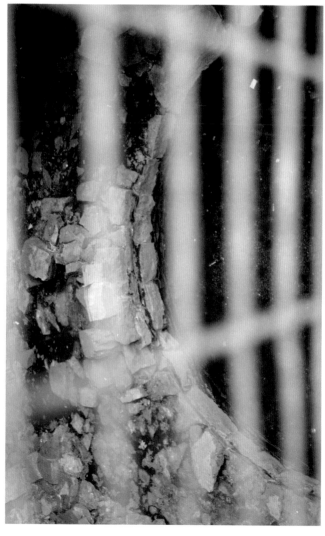

t's an Irish solution to an Irish problem. During the development of a new apartment complex, the foundations of a cornerstone of Dublin's 13th-century city walls are discovered. What to do? Why, after an admirable excavation, you build around and above them, of course – leaving passers-by to view the neglected results in a dank basement pit through a rusty metal grid.

But here's the thing. Despite its shameful presentation (beer cans and cigarette butts are scattered throughout the stagnant pond), Isolde's Tower still sucks you in. The more you stare into that dankness, the more you see. Discovered in 1993 during an archeological dig on behalf of Temple Bar Properties, the foundations belong to a tower built as part of an extension to the city walls in Anglo-Norman Dublin. The tower is 4m thick, and though the surviving stones stand at barely half that height, you can still get a sense of the seriousness of any potential attack from the River Liffey. In its heyday, the tower projected into the river at up to 12m in height, serving as a first line of defence – not to mention a grisly backdrop for the display of criminals' heads on spikes. Along with a range of post-medieval pottery, several skulls were discovered in river silt during the excavation.

Isolde's Tower is named for the daughter of the sixth-century King Aonghus – her ill-fated love for an English lord inspired the legend of Tristan and Iseult (or Isolde). It was demolished in the late 17th century – ironically, another period during which Dublin's medieval defences were hindering its 'modern' development. Its foundations lay buried until discovered during excavations for the soulless bank of apartments in whose bowels they skulk on today's Exchange Street Lower. As Dublin City Council does not control the site, its hands have been tied in arresting its deterioration – the 'exhibit' is regularly blocked by wheelie bins, and a thoughtful set of railings designed by artist Grace Weir has been allowed to rust. The tower itself is regularly flooded. Sigh!

The story of soap

Parliament Street & Essex Quay, Dublin 2
Tara Street DART station (5-min. walk); Luas, Jervis Street (Red Line;
5-min. walk); Dublin Bus stops 1443, 1479 and 2912 are nearby

Stand at the south-east corner of Grattan Bridge and look back towards the corner of Parliament Street and Essex Quay. Block out the trundling Dublin buses, perhaps the duvet of grey sky overhead and you could – just for a moment – be in mercantile Italy.

The building facing you, Sunlight Chambers, is one of the most unusual in Dublin. Dating from 1901, it was designed by Edward Ould (the architect of Liverpool's Port Sunlight) in Italianate style and is most notable for the ceramic friezes between storeys: sunny splashes of colour crafted by the sculptor and potter, Conrad Dressler. From a distance, you'd assume the friezes depict classical scenes. But no. The building was constructed as the Irish headquarters of Lever Brothers, the British soap and detergent manufacturers (Sunlight was one of its brands at the time) and the terracotta curiosities pay homage to the art of a good scrub. Look closely, and you'll see washerwomen cleaning

clothes, merchants haggling for oils and smellies, labourers ploughing fields, women drawing water from a well. 'The story of soap', as it has been described, is quite the counterpoint to dear old dirty Dublin.

Above the friezes, the building's overhanging eaves are unlike any of its neighbours'. There's also a tiled roof and the top two storeys are arcaded. Apparently, Sunlight Chambers met with opposition from Irish architects and builders at the time (Ould was British), with *The Irish Builder* journal dubbing it the ugliest building in Dublin. This is hardly the case, but as Lisa Cassidy points out in her 'Built Dublin' blog, Sunlight Chambers isn't all squeaky-clean. The forced labour used to extract palm oil in the Belgian Congo – a key ingredient in Lever Brothers' products – doesn't conjure up scenes quite as rosy as those unfolding across the friezes. According to Jules Marchal's book, *Lord Leverhulme's Ghosts* (Verso, 2008), forced labour reduced the population of the colony by half, accounting for more deaths than the Holocaust.

Today, the building is occupied by M. E. Hanahoe solicitors, who commissioned a complete restoration in the late 1990s. Architects Gilroy McMahon consulted widely in conserving and cleaning up the stone and ceramics, resulting in the beautiful colours of today.

THE RIVER PODDLE

Dublin's underground river

Wellington Quay, Dublin 2
Tara Street, DART station (15-min. walk); Luas, Jervis Street (Red Line;
5–10-min. walk); Dublin Bus stops 312 and 1479 are nearby on the quays

The River Liffey is Dublin's iconic waterway, flowing through the city centre and cleaving apart its great north–south divide. But there are other rivers coursing through the cityscape, including one running almost entirely underground: the River Poddle.

The best way to catch a glimpse of Dublin's shyest river is to stand on the boardwalk at Ormond Quay. Looking across the Liffey towards Wellington Quay, you'll make out a small arched opening in the quay wall, guarded by a murky, weed-strewn gate. This is the main outfall for the Poddle and is best viewed at low tide, when you get the full effect of its trickle emerging from the tunnel. The Poddle wasn't always hidden, of course. In medieval times, the river formed the moat around Dublin Castle, converging with the Liffey in a tidal pool at the site of today's Dubh Linn Gardens. This 'black pool' is where the Vikings are likely to have moored their ships, and of course, it gave the city its name. Rising in Cookstown and flowing through Tempelogue and Kimmage before it hit the medieval city centre, the Poddle was an important source of fresh water for the developing city, and its estuary (which would have covered the area around Crane Lane and Essex Street in today's Temple Bar) remained a feature of the cityscape until it first began to be filled and culverted in the early 17th century.

This twisting, turning subterranean river is central to Dublin's heritage and lore. In 1592 it aided Red Hugh O'Donnell's escape from Dublin Castle. The Poddle is also believed to be the same 'River Sáile' from the ballad made famous by The Dubliners. 'Salach' is an Irish word meaning 'dirty', which would have been a good description of the river before it was fully enclosed during the 18th and 19th centuries. Today, fully 4km of the river is culverted, and though not publicly accessible, you can follow its course above ground from Ship Street to Palace Street, where it bifurcates, with one channel passing under the Olympia Theatre, before reuniting once again to exit the brick tunnel at Wellington Quay.

GUITAR, RORY GALLAGHER CORNER

④

It's got a kind of tattoo quality about it …

Temple Bar, Dublin 2
Tara Street DART station (5–10-min. walk); Dublin Bus stop 312 is nearby
on Wellington Quay

Blues legend Rory Gallagher (1948–95) inspired huge devotion, both during his life and after. In fact, were you so inclined, you could undertake a Rory Gallagher-themed tour of the country. Think of the bronze statue and tribute festivals in his hometown of Ballyshannon, Co. Donegal, his grave in Ballincollig, Co. Cork, or the site of Crowley's Music Shop – where Gallagher bought his famous Fender Stratocaster, a 1961 Sunburst model that was reputedly the first in Ireland.

That Stratocaster has since been retired by Rory's brother, Donal Gallagher, but you can find a copy of it in a rather unusual place: attached to the wall on the corner of Meeting House Square and Essex Street in Temple Bar. The intersection here has been known as Rory Gallagher Corner since the area was developed, but it wasn't until the mid-noughties that a planning application was lodged on behalf of Dublin's music equipment stores to erect a memorial to the Donegal musician. Dublin City Council gave its blessing in 2006, and despite fears that the corner would become a shrine for fans who couldn't resist showering it with graffiti, it's been respected ever since.

The original guitar is almost as famous as the bluesman himself. Gallagher picked his Fender (serial no. 64351) second-hand after its first owner – a showband guitarist – returned it because he had ordered red. 'It was in good condition when I bought it, but it's got so battered now it's got a kind of tattoo quality about it,' Gallagher later said. 'There's now a theory that the less paint or varnish on a guitar, acoustic or electric, the better. The wood breathes more. But it's all psychological. I just like the sound of it.' The Strat was stolen from the back of a tour van in 1961 (the theft featured on RTÉ's *Garda Patrol*), but despite lying abandoned in a ditch for days, it suffered no lasting damage.

According to Gallagher's official website, rorygallagher.com, the guitar's wear and tear (faithfully reproduced in bronze on this Temple Bar street corner) was partly due to the high acidic content of its owner's rare blood group. 'So when Rory sweated on stage – and he sweated buckets – it was like paint stripper.'

Fender has since made a tribute model of the priceless instrument.

THE STONE WALLS OF POWERSCOURT TOWNHOUSE

That stone is actually wood …

South William Street, Dublin 2
powerscourtcentre.ie
Monday–Saturday 10am–6pm, Sunday 12noon–6pm
Pearse and Tara Street DART stations are about a 10-min walk away; Many buses stop nearby on South Great Georges Street, while the Luas Green Line stops at Stephen's Green

Powerscourt Townhouse feels like a treasure chest, at once a boutique shopping mall crammed with some of the loveliest antiques, fashion and craft jewellery shops (not to mention the best sandwiches) in the city, and a heritage gem modestly billed as 'the third finest Georgian house in Dublin'.

Scale the granite steps to the entrance hall, originally quarried from the Powerscourt Estate in County Wicklow, and you'll step into a blooming flower shop in the foyer. Look down – the Kilkenny marble and limestone beneath your feet comprises the only trompe l'oeil floor in Dublin. Next, step into interiors store Article, and look up. The ceiling's arabesque plasterwork once crowned the dressing room of Richard Wingfield, the third Viscount Powerscourt (1744–1788). After that, take a spin up the lavish staircase and its hall, where styles bridge freehand rococo and restrained neoclassical. Take note of the way its banister ends in a 'monkey's tail', and tap your knuckles on the creamy, well-proportioned 'stone' walls as you wind up the stairs. The hollow sound reveals their true material – wood.

The house began life in the 1770s as a city residence for the viscount. His stunning Palladian mansion in Enniskerry was the family's principal residence, but they decamped to Dublin during the 'season' – described in a display here as the time for Parliament, balls and banquets. Interestingly, the townhouse wasn't designed by an architect, but by stonemason Robert Mack (he didn't do a bad job), and originally included formal gardens to the rear, as well as an observatory in the attic. After the Act of Union, the mansion housed the Government Stamp Office, and additional buildings and the courtyard were added by Francis Johnson, the Board of Works architect best known for the GPO on O'Connell Street. Another chapter in its history saw the building spend 100 years as home to wholesale drapers, Ferrier Pollock.

Today's transformation is a treat, given how many of Dublin's architectural treasures we know have been lost or trashed by developers. A photo in the hall shows the courtyard in 1978, before its metamorphosis – crammed with parked cars. Just 10 years later, it had emerged from its chrysalis.

'WHY GO BALD' SIGN

Bono's favourite Dublin landmark

3 South Great George's Street, Dublin 2
Bus Stops 1934 and 7581; Tara Street DART station is a 10-min walk

Dublin's 'Why go Bald' sign is an icon and an irreplaceable piece of street furniture to some, but completely unknown to others. It blends into the clutter of signage on its Dame Lane corner building by day, but pops to life by night, when bright yellow, red and orange neon lights flash to reveal a svelte blond man with what look likes thin needles of light either emanating from, or shooting into, his head. In true Dublin fashion, it's at once completely ordinary and ridiculously endearing. It's been made into posters and prints, featured in an Electric Ireland TV ad, at one point had its own Facebook page, and is popularly held to be Bono's favourite Dublin landmark. In 2012, in the depths of Ireland's post-Celtic Tiger financial crisis, *Totally Dublin* even listed it at No.80 on its '200 reasons not to leave Dublin'.

'Along with the video screen showing ads above Centra', it wrote, 'the Why Go Bald sign on Dame Lane is part of Ireland's Times Square, asking us all an important question nightly with its neon glow.'

The sign was made by Taylor Signs in the early 1960s as an ad for the Universal Hair & Scalp Clinic, which has been serving the follically challenged citizens of Dublin for over 60 years. 'We had problems about the sign at first', Ann Goldsmith of the Clinic once told *The Irish Times*. 'The Corporation said it would be a distraction, but we fought and got permission eventually.'

Over the years, it has appeared in movies including *A Man of No Importance* and *Educating Rita*, but was almost lost to disrepair in the 1990s, before being saved by a restoration carried out by the company that made it. The lights came back on in 1999, an event reported by RTE news. In recent years, it has also received modest grants under the Built Heritage Investment Scheme (BHIS), a government fund supporting owners and custodians of historic and protected structures in maintaining their properties.

Much like a gentleman's hairline, this isn't a static sign. Watch closely as its routine plays out. First, the lights show the young man with a full head of hair. Next, disaster strikes as a clean arc shoots across his pate. Finally, those radiant beams (and a big smile) complete the narrative arc. It's quirky, clever, slightly silly, definitely cheesy, and by now, pure Dublin.

But why is its question posed without a question mark?

STAG'S HEAD MOSAIC ⑦

You couldn't buy advertising like it

Dame Court, Dame Street,
Dublin 2
01 679-3687
louisfitzgerald.com (Stag's Head)
Tara Street DART station (5–10-min. walk); Luas, St Stephen's Green (Green
Line; 5–10-min. walk); Dublin Bus stops 1358 and 1278 are nearby

As welcome mats go, this is rather special. Strolling along Dame Street, look down as you pass the covert little alleyway opposite the Central Bank. A colourful mosaic of a stag's head is set into the pavement, with a stark black arrow directing you towards Dame Court. Follow that arrow down the rabbit hole and you'll end up at the Stag's Head pub.

Although there have been taverns on this street corner since the late 1700s, the Stag's Head dates in its current form from 1895, when businessman George Tyson planned a Victorian pub that might compare favourably 'with the best establishments of its kind either in London or any other part of England,' as Turtle Bunbury writes in *The Irish Pub* (Thames & Hudson). Its regular customers – a motley mix of blow-ins, Trinity College students, theatre types and suits from the nearby stock exchange – would surely agree that he succeeded. Behind the redbrick façade lies a gorgeously opulent time capsule, with an original Aberdeen granite bar, studded banquettes, bevelled mirrors, ancient whiskey casks, a whispery snug (the old Victorian 'Smoke Room') and mahogany panelling all contributing atmospherics. Oh, and just in case you need reminding of where you are, there's a colossal stag's head mounted over the main bar, and several colourful animals set into the pub's stained glass panels and lamps.

The Stag's Head has its stories, of course – like the time Quentin Tarantino is said to have been refused service for pulling rank. He wasn't the only Hollywood star to visit – *Educating Rita* (1983) and *A Man of No Importance* (1994) were filmed here too. The pub has even featured on a postage stamp.

The original Dame Street mosaic was removed for refurbishment in the early noughties, prompting an outcry from those who noticed. Thankfully, it has since been returned to its rightful place, though eagle-eyed Dubliners might notice that it is now a little further from the alley and the 'wrong' way round. The none-too-subtle arrow is also a new addition. The alley is as grotty as the pub is grand (you can skip the puke and pee by taking the long way around via South Great George's Street), but let's not quibble over minor details. There's gold at the end of the rainbow, however you get there.

SICK & INDIGENT
ROOMKEEPERS' SOCIETY

Dublin's oldest surviving charity

2 Palace Street,
Dublin 2
roomkeepers.com
Tara Street DART station (10–15-min. walk); Luas, St Stephen's Green (Green
Line; 15-min. walk); Dublin Bus stops 1934, 1935 and 2003 are nearby

The late 1700s may have been a golden age for architecture in Dublin, but they also saw some desperate poverty and squalor – with countless families in the inner city crammed into appalling conditions rife with filth, disease and little prospect of improvement.

The Sick & Indigent Roomkeepers' Society was established in 1790 to alleviate the plight of Dubliners who had fallen ill or become destitute through no fault of their own. In the absence of a system of public welfare, this motley crew of concerned citizens – including grocers, a schoolmaster, a stonecutter, a carpenter and a pawnbroker in their ranks – developed a fund to relieve 'the honest poor', as *The Irish Times* later termed them, providing temporary aid in the form of fuel, rent, tools or equipment. It was a successful initiative, with donations swelling to the point where it became one of the leading charities of the 19th century – organising balls, temperance picnics and, in 1855, moving into these striking premises, set just a few metres from the pedestrian entrance to Dublin Castle on Palace Street.

The building itself is a Georgian gem, the only surviving 18th-century structure on the street (apart from the castle gate), and one with a knack for surprising Dubliners who stumble across it. Although the charity vacated No. 2 for smaller offices on Leeson Street in the late 1990s (it is now based on Fitzwilliam Square), its name remains emblazoned in bold and quirky letters across the facade, striking a contrasting note to the cosy Chez Max bistro tucked away beside it. As well as its charitable history, the house is a former home of Irish State physician Robert Emmet, whose son and namesake was executed after a failed rebellion in 1803. The British military occupied it in 1921, and recently, its unusual appeal was echoed in the name of Americana-influenced Dublin band, The Sick and Indigent Song Club.

The Sick & Indigent Roomkeepers' Society is the oldest surviving charity in the city, although operations have scaled back significantly since its heyday. No. 2 has also been home to architectural historian and painter, Peter Pearson, who was instrumental in its restoration.

CITY HALL MURALS

A hidden history of Dublin

City Hall, Dame Street, Dublin 2
01 222-2204
dublincity.ie/dublincityhall
Monday–Saturday 10am–4pm
Admission: free
Tara Street DART station (10-min. walk); Dublin Bus stop 1934 is on Dame Street nearby

Most cities tell their stories in words. And Lord knows, Dublin – one of a handful of UNESCO Cities of Literature – is no slouch in that regard. But did you know that its story is told in pictures too? Step into the rotunda of City Hall and look up. As your eyes adapt to the light, you'll make out 12 panels under the ornate dome depicting historic scenes and the heraldic arms of the provinces.

The murals, measuring about 2.5x1.2m, were proposed by James Ward in 1913. Ward was head of the Dublin Metropolitan School of Art and he saw the project as a way to gain some hands-on experience for his students. Permission was granted by Dublin Corporation with the proviso that the subject matter relate to the history of the city (which it did). Eight, now slightly murky, figurative panels portray key legends and scenes from Dublin's past. In 'Irishmen oppose the landing of the Viking fleet 841AD', for example, a stoic central figure rallies his troops as Scandinavian longships approach. 'Brian Boru addressing his army before the Battle of Clontarf 1014AD' stresses Ireland's Catholic heritage. It depicts Boru on horseback, bearing a small crucifix with a milky-hued Jesus slumped on its wood. Boru himself looks like Gandalf the White.

All the subjects are medieval, which doubtless protected them from political controversy at the time, but they are of course open to interpretation. It's easy to see struggles with Viking invaders, for instance, as echoing the conflicts under English rule. City Hall is no Sistine Chapel, but the more you absorb yourself in the murals, the more layers they reveal ... even if Ward's students didn't always feel the same way. Indeed, a young Harry Clarke – as Philip McEvansoneya wrote in *The Irish Arts Review* – is said to have grown 'heartily sick' of the tedious and time-consuming nature of the work.

City Hall was built between 1769 and 1779 as the Royal Exchange – a financial hub for the city's merchants. Dublin Corporation purchased the building in 1851 and it went on to host the funerals of Charles Stewart Parnell and Michael Collins, among others – even doing a stint as temporary HQ of the Irish Provisional Government. In the vaults, you'll find 'The Story of the Capital', an interactive exhibition tracing the history of the city from Viking and Norman times to the present day.

LADY JUSTICE

Justice is blind … or is it?

Dublin Castle,
Dublin 2
Tara Street DART station (10–15-min. walk); Luas, St Stephen's Green
(Green Line; 5-min. walk); Dublin Bus stop 1934 is nearby

Lady Justice has some very simple symbolism to get right. Personifying justice, she must hold a sword and a balanced set of scales representing truth and fairness. She should face the people. And she is often blindfolded, representing her impartiality and her ability to make judgments without regard for class, wealth or identity.

So why does Dublin's old dear get it so wrong? Standing atop the entrance to Dublin Castle's upper yard off Castle Street, just beside the 18th-century Bedford Tower, Lady Justice shows her back to the city. Her eyes are wide open. Look closely and you may even notice that her scales are tipped ever-so-slightly to one side.

The statue has been controversial, it turns out, ever since John Van Nost sculpted it at the behest of the British authorities in 1751. 'The Lady Justice, consider her station, her face to the castle, her arse to the nation,' is the popular saying. And while the leaning scales may be explained by rain dripping down the statue's arm into one of the pans, there's a rather delicious irony in the fact that they lean towards the side of the castle housing the tax offices, as the excellent city blog Come Here To Me (comeheretome.com) points out. Nor will it be lost on Dubliners that Lady Justice looks over both the historic centre of administration in the city, and the site of the famous tribunals of inquiry into corrupt payments to politicians.

Perhaps her smile shows a little more insight and wisdom than she is credited with.

CHESTER BEATTY ROOF GARDEN ⑪

An oasis of calm in the city centre

Chester Beatty, Dublin Castle, Dublin 2
01 407-0750
cbl.ie
March–October: Monday–Friday 10am–5pm, Saturday 11am–5pm, Sunday 1pm–5pm; November–February: Tuesday–Friday 10am–5pm, Saturday 11am–5pm, Sunday 1pm–5pm; Closed Monday
Admission: free
Tara Street DART station (10–15-min. walk); Luas, Stephen's Green (Green Line; 5-min. walk); Dublin Bus stop 1934 is nearby

Understandably for a city that is rained upon so often, Dublin doesn't really 'do' roof gardens. That's not to say roof gardens are not 'done', of course – as this peachy patch atop the Chester Beatty in Dublin Castle attests.

The rooftop garden is an oasis of calm in a busy city centre. Split into a series of different surfaces – gravel, ornamental grasses, stone and hardwood – the small space commands some lovely views over the Dubh Linn Gardens below, and the sprawl of Dublin Castle beyond. Freely accessible through the museum (though backpacks, food and cameras must be checked), its close-knit timber trellises give the feeling as much of a fancy backyard as a rooftop project. The plants creeping

up these wooden barriers are slowly transforming them into green walls, though the carefully positioned 'windows' will remain, preserving the bird's-eye views over the cityscape. Creative use of indigenous materials creates the overall sense of a contemporary Irish garden, but there's also a Japanese feel to the layout, with its emphasis on harmony and lack of a single dominating feature. Wisteria, silver birch, honeysuckle, bamboo, clematis and heather are just some of the plants adding colour. It's the perfect setting for The Chester Beatty's Qigong classes, too!

Beneath this rooftop oasis lies Dublin's most under-appreciated museum. The Chester Beatty may be 'one of the finest small museums in the world', according to *The Washington Post*, but locals have been slower to give it a go. Step inside the door, however, and you're hooked. Beatty's collection of manuscripts, prints, icons, miniatures, early printed books and objets d'art is considered the most valuable gift ever given to the Irish nation, with Chinese jade books, dragon robes worn by emperors, papyrus gospels dating from AD 150, clay tablets from Babylon and the earliest known copies of the Book of Revelation just some of the highlights. Throw in a surprising menu of Middle Eastern food at the Silk Road Café, not to mention a beautifully airy atrium, and you have the makings of a very interesting afternoon.

OUR LADY OF DUBLIN

The Black Madonna of Dublin

Whitefriar Street Church (original)
56 Aungier Street, Dublin 2
01 475-8821; whitefriarstreetchurch.ie
Monday–Friday 8am–6pm, Sunday 8am–7.30pm
Admission: free
Tara Street DART station (20-min. walk); Luas, Harcourt Street (Green Line; 10-min. walk); Dublin Bus stop 1354 is close to the church on Aungier Street

The Church of Our Lady of Mount Carmel ('Whitefriar' stems from the white cloaks worn by the Carmelites, who were first recorded here in 1274) is home to a fascinating collection of shrines and memorabilia. Most fascinating of all is that dedicated to Our Lady of Dublin.

At its heart is a 16th-century oak statue of the Virgin Mary and the Infant Jesus, its blackened colour offset by an explosion of golden mosaic tiles and white marble. The statue is originally believed to have belonged to St Mary's Abbey, a wealthy Cistercian monastery that played a central role in the affairs of the State until its dissolution under Henry VIII. A statue of the Madonna comparable to some of the contemporary pieces at Westminster Abbey's Henry VII Chapel is said to have held pride of place in the abbey's church. When St Mary's was surrendered, tradition has it that the statue was disguised as a pig trough in a nearby inn yard to avoid detection. This isn't as unlikely as it sounds: statues of the period were commonly hollowed-out to reduce their weight and prevent warping and splitting of the wood.

The mysterious Madonna next found a home in a chapel on St Mary's Lane, as the story goes, before making its way to a second-hand shop on Capel Street. There, it was spotted by the Carmelite, Fr John Spratt, and brought to Whitefriar Street in 1824. The statue is said to be the only one of its kind in Dublin to have escaped destruction following the Reformation, although Our Lady's jewel-bedecked headpiece was not part of the purchase – the original silver crown ('a double-arched crown such as appears on the coins of Henry VII') is believed to have been sold and melted down.

As well as its many shrines, Whitefriar Street Church houses several displays in its entrance corridor, including the story of Noel Purcell's famous words, uttered to a Carmelite priest as he lay on his deathbed at the Adelaide Hospital: 'Tell the Gaffer that Purcell is ready when He is.'

ST VALENTINE'S RELICS & THE BLESSING OF THE RINGS

Love's final resting place

Whitefriar Street Church, 56 Aungier Street,
Dublin 2
01 475-8821; whitefriarstreetchurch.ie
Monday–Friday 8am–6pm, Sunday 8am–7.30pm
Admission: free
Dublin Bus stop 4456 is at the Carmelite priory on Aungier Street

You can look for love anywhere, but the odds of finding it are that bit higher at a rather unexpected location: the Church of Our Lady of Mount Carmel. Better known as the Whitefriar Street Church, one of its shrines contains a life-size statue of a saint, together with his relics.

His name? St Valentine.

The brass inscription is beautifully matter-of-fact. 'This shrine contains the sacred body of Saint Valentinus the Martyr,' it reads. 'Together with a small vessel tinged with his blood.' The relics are contained in a small wooden box tied with a red silk ribbon and sealed with wax. The box is contained within a casket bearing the papal coat of arms of Gregory XVI. The casket is contained within a glass display in a marble alcove. The inner box remains unopened.

So how did St Valentine end up in Dublin? In 1835 John Spratt paid a visit to Rome. The Irish Carmelite's reputation as a preacher preceded him, so when he spoke at the famous Church of the Gesù, the elite of Rome flocked to hear him and offer tokens of their esteem. Intriguingly, one such token came from Pope Gregory XVI himself: the remains of St Valentine. The remains had been 'taken out of the cemetery of St Hippolytus in the Tiburtine Way,' according to a plaque on the casket, and they arrived in Dublin on 10 November 1836. Although placed in storage for a time after Fr Spratt's death, a shrine was constructed in the 1950s, complete with a carved statue of the saint.

Today's shrine is found in a little alcove to the right of the altar. On and around it, look out for little notes and cards left by visitors – the church has also at times left a notebook in which people can write their petitions. 'Thank you for helping Natalie and I sort out our troubles,' read one on a Secret Dublin visit, with a smiley-face after the name. 'I'm never going to let her go. I love her forever and ever.' Other entries asked St Valentine to bless their families, to help couples looking for a home and to intercede for lonely souls in their search for company.

On St Valentine's Day, couples are also welcome to attend a ceremony that includes a blessing of rings. Every 14 February, the reliquary is removed from the shrine and placed before the high altar; afterwards, you can buy a little souvenir at the shop by the entrance.

ST KEVIN'S PARK

The perfect place to bring a book ...
or a body-snatcher

Camden Row, Dublin 8
dublincity.ie
Daylight hours
Admission: free
Tara Street DART station (20-min. walk); Luas, Charlemont or Harcourt
Street (Green Line; 5-min. walk); Dublin Bus stops 1285 and 1353 are nearby
on Wexford Street

Dublin has its well-known parks and its lesser-known parks. St Kevin's is definitely one of the latter, a leafy little oasis set in a former churchyard off Wexford Street. It's a gorgeous little pocket of peace, no more than a stone's throw from the perky pubs, venues and restaurants of Wexford Street. The snoozing local or office worker spotted here with a book or a sandwich always looks like the cat that got the cream.

Though St Kevin's is a small park, it's not that tiny – there's plenty of space for strolling and sitting along the lawns and pathways under its ash, yew, birch and elder trees. At its heart is the shell of an 18th-century church where Arthur Wellesley, the first Duke of Wellington, is said to have been baptised – though the only new life in evidence today is hidden away in the thatch of ivy covering its limestone, where birds nest and late summer and autumn flowers provide nectar for bees, butterflies and wasps. Indeed, 19 bird and three bat species have been spotted here, according to Dublin City Council's Parks Division.

In spite of the teeming wildlife, the park's cemetery contains plenty of death. By now, most of its gravestones have been stacked upright against perimeter walls, but several of the more prominent examples remain in situ, including that of Thomas Moore's family. In the church, a secret grave is said to mark the burial place of Archbishop Dermot O'Hurley, a religious figure hanged for treason in 1584 after enduring horrific torture. A memorial at the south-east corner of the building goes into some detail: '[This] included roasting the archbishop's legs in two boots filled with boiling pitch and oil.' Perhaps O'Hurley is resting more easily since his beatification by Pope John Paul II in 1992.

Like many old city cemeteries, St Kevin's was targeted by body-snatchers – opportunistic grave robbers who stole freshly buried corpses to supply city medical schools in the decades leading up to the Anatomy Act of 1831. Rumour has it that the souls whose headstones were rearranged have stayed to haunt the place.

IRISH JEWISH MUSEUM

Portobello was once known as 'Little Jerusalem'

3 Walworth Road, Dublin 8
089-426-3625 ; jewishmuseum.ie
May–September: Sunday, Monday, Tuesday, Wednesday & Thursday
11am–3pm; October–April: Sunday 10.30am–2.30pm
Group bookings by arrangement
Admission: free
Luas (Green Line) stops at Charlemont Place and Harcourt Street, both a
10–15-min. walk away. Several Dublin Bus routes stop at nearby Richmond
Street South and Rathmines Road Lower

Ireland's Jewish community reached its peak in the 1940s, with some 5,000 members. Today, that number has fallen to around 1,500, according to an Irish Jewish Museum that provides a fusty but fascinating insight into their heritage in the heart of Portobello. Wentworth Road, with its Victorian redbricks, feels like an unlikely location for a museum – but Portobello was once known as 'Little Jerusalem' and hummed with synagogues, schools, homes and kosher businesses (the Bretzel Bakery survives on nearby Lennox Street, albeit under new management). At No. 3, a modest red doorway bears an intercom that visitors are invited to 'Please Ring': inside, you'll find a ground floor crammed with display cases and a restored, first-floor synagogue strewn with ark covers and

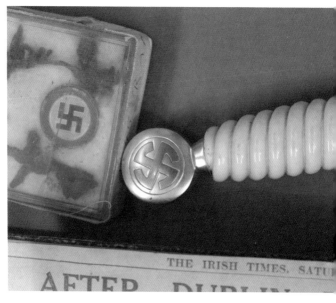

Torah scrolls. At first, it all feels a bit stuffy and dated, but the more moseying and nosing about you do, the more intimate it becomes. A curator's letter welcoming visitors dates from 1989. Yellowing election posters, photographs and news clippings recall well-known Dublin politicians like Robert Briscoe and his son Ben, or Mervyn Taylor. There are identity cards, mementos of old Jewish businesses, a wooden Victorian shopping basket and a recreated kitchen – complete with two separate sinks and draining boards for meat and dairy. A display devoted to James Joyce's *Ulysses* also highlights the fact that Leopold Bloom was a Jew, born on Upper Clanbrassil Street.

A case of World War II artefacts makes a deep impression. Among other items, it contains a yellow Star of David arm patch; a copy of the marriage certificate of Ester Steinberg, the only known Irish victim of the Holocaust; pieces of bomb shrapnel recovered from the damaged Greenville Hall Synagogue; and a Nazi dagger with brass swastika and ivory handle. On closer inspection, this chilling keepsake turns out to bear a hopeful inscription – as an accompanying *Irish Times* article explains. It was gifted to the museum by Moris Block, a Jewish Dubliner who served with the British Army and spent the final days of the war in Dusseldorf. There, he helped three German Jews who had spent much of the war hiding in a basement, and one of them inscribed the dagger as a thank-you. 'To my friend Moris Block in memory A Fischmann', it reads, alongside a Star of David dated 1945.

IVEAGH GARDENS

One of Dublin's best-kept secrets

Clonmel Street, off Harcourt Street, Dublin 2 (main entrance)
iveaghgardens.ie
Monday–Saturday 8am, Sunday & Bank Holidays 10am;
Gates close at 3.30pm (December & January), 4pm (November & February),
7.30pm (March–October)
Admission: free
Luas (Green Line) stops at Stephen's Green nearby

They're just a few hundred yards from Stephen's Green. In summer, they host concerts attended by thousands. The dogs on the street know them. Yet somehow, the Iveagh Gardens remain one of Dublin's best-kept secrets.

Why? One answer is their invisibility. Though not much smaller than Stephen's Green, the gardens' access points are well hidden – through small gates stashed away behind the National Concert Hall, on Hatch Street, and behind an old house on Clonmel Street, for example. Wander off the beaten track, however, and you're soon rewarded with a gorgeous and leafy arrangement of sunken lawns and set pieces – from waterfalls and fountains to short, squirrel-spotted woodland walks, rockeries, a rustic grotto and cascade, a rosarium whose collection dates back over 150 years, and a sundial within a souvenir-sized yew maze … all less than five minutes on foot from Grafton Street.

The Iveagh Gardens began life as part of 'Leeson's Fields', an uncultivated swathe of land fanning out south of the mansion once owned by the wealthy Leeson family. After Harcourt Street was laid out in the late 18th century, the Earl of Clonmell bought 11 acres of the fields as a garden for his house (today's No. 17) – a subterranean passage built between house and gardens is still believed to exist. The gardens

fell in and out of favour while leased for public use in the early 19th century, before being bought by Benjamin Lee Guinness as a garden for his townhouse (Iveagh House, on Stephen's Green), and transformed into their current layout by landscape gardener Ninian Niven ahead of the Great Exhibition of 1865.

A subsequent Lord Iveagh gifted them to the Irish state and, thankfully, any temptation to build on this lovely city 'lung' has been resisted. To this day, trivia fans may be tickled to know that the sunken lawn remains the only purpose-built archery ground in the country.

IRISH MARBLE PANELS

Rock 'n' Roll at the Department of Justice

Dept of Justice & Equality, 51 St Stephen's Green, Dublin 2
01 674-4999
justice.ie
Office hours
Admission: free
Pearse Street DART station (5–10-min. walk); Dublin Bus stops 843 and 844
are close to No. 51 St Stephen's Green East

If you're looking for justice, 51 St Stephen's Green may or may not deliver. If you're looking for a surprise collection of Irish marble, on the other hand, then the lobby of the Department of Justice and Equality comes through every time.

The building itself sits on the site of the 17th-century residence of the Monck family. It was rebuilt around 1760 by George Paul Monck, as an information handout explains (Rocque's maps of 1756 and 1773 describe this side of the Green as Monks' Walk). In the early 1800s it came to be known as the Lord Chancellor's House after it was acquired by Lord Mannors, a former Lord Chancellor of Ireland. In 1848, 51 St Stephen's Green was purchased by the government and turned into a Museum of Irish Industry, and it's from this period that the 40 samples of Irish marble in the lobby appear to date. They arrived thanks to museum director Sir Robert Kane, who wished 'to promote the commercial potential of Ireland's quarries and natural resources', as Mary Mulvihill wrote in her offbeat guide to the city, *Ingenious Ireland*.

The range of colours used in the panels is quietly breathtaking and certainly succeeds in showcasing the variety of Irish stone. Not all of it is marble, however. There are sleek black samples from Kilkenny, evocative of night skies pinpricked with stars. There is pale green Connemara marble, rippling with the echoes of ancient geological forces. But fully 34 of the panels are in fact polished limestone. The secret is out …

HUGUENOT CEMETERY

A surprise cemetery ...

27 St Stephen's Green, Dublin 2
Pearse Street DART station (10 min. walk); Luas, St Stephen's Green (5 min. walk); Dublin Bus stop 768 is directly outside the Huguenot cemetery on Merrion Row

Merrion Row is a short strip of prime Dublin real estate, stretching from the Shelbourne Hotel at one end to Doheny & Nesbitt's pub at the other. That's why, hemmed in between two modern office buildings, it's such a surprise to find a gate bearing the inscription: 'Huguenot Cemetery, 1693'. Beyond the gate, colourful trees drip down over the decaying headstones. In spring, the plots are covered in a carpet of bluebells, making the city-centre scene even more unlikely.

The Huguenots were French Protestants who fled their country after the Edict of Nantes (1598) was revoked in 1685. The edict had promoted a more tolerant approach by a Catholic country to Calvinists and other minority religious communities, but was rolled back by Louis XIV, prompting an exodus. Sensing an opportunity, James Butler, the first Duke of Ormonde and Lord Lieutenant of Ireland, extended an invitation, hoping that Ireland's economy would benefit from Huguenot skills and industry. This it did, as new arrivals quickly became a dynamic community in Dublin. Settling in the Liberties, they soon enjoyed commercial success in textiles, finance, wine importation, watch-making and other businesses, supplemented by a reputation for integrity … as attested by the saying, 'As honest as a Huguenot'.

The cemetery became a designated French burial ground in 1693. Its gates are now closed to visitors, but it's so small you can see everything through the railings anyway, including the inscriptions on several graves, and a large marble panel naming 240 or so souls buried within – if not quite from A to Z, then at least from Afée to Plantier de Montvert. Du Bédat is a name that crops up in James Joyce's *Ulysses*. 'Wouldn't mind being a waiter in a swell hotel,' Bloom daydreams. 'Tips, evening dress, halfnaked ladies. May I tempt you to a little more filleted lemon sole, miss Dubedat? Yes, do bedad. And she did bedad. Huguenot name I expect that.' Though Joyce would certainly have been familiar with the cemetery, it's hard to say if this plot inspired that particular rumination, however. There are Du Bedat tombs in Mount Jerome also.

The Huguenot cemetery closed in 1901. After falling into ruin in the 1980s, it was restored by the French Ministry of Foreign Affairs and is today cared for by Dublin City Council. Before you leave, check the inscription, where Huguenot is misspelled as 'Hughenot'. Joycean pun or stonemason's mistake?

THE SHELBOURNE'S SECRET MUSEUM

A five-star time capsule

27 St Stephen's Green, Dublin 2
01 663-4500
theshelbourne.com
Restricted to hotel guests and customers
Pearse Street DART station (10-min walk); Luas, St Stephen's Green (5-min walk); Dublin Bus stop 768 is directly outside the Huguenot cemetery on Merrion Row

The Shelbourne Hotel is one of Dublin's grande dame institutions, a sparkling old Georgian building on the corner of St Stephen's Green. That much is obvious.

The history hidden within these walls is more of a mystery. Sure, we all know that the Irish Constitution was drafted here in 1922, in Room 112, under the chairmanship of Michael Collins. You may also know that Peter O'Toole once bathed in champagne at the hotel and that celebrity guests have ranged from Charlie Chaplin to JFK, Michelle Obama, Grace Kelly and the Rolling Stones. But were you aware that, squirrelled away in the lift lobby next to reception, there is a tiny museum dedicated to its history?

Well, maybe 'museum' is a generous word. Prior to the hotel's recent refurbishment, this was a slightly larger space with more items on display. But artefacts have been lovingly laid out in several small displays opposite the elevators and they tell some tantalising tales. They can be visited by guests of the hotel (or customers enjoying, say, afternoon tea in the Lord Mayor's Lounge, dinner in the Saddle Room or cocktails in the bar).

A quick perusal here evokes some of glittering moments since the hotel opened in 1824. Look for the photo of Ronnie Drew and The Dubliners, for instance, or the chambermaid making up a bed – set behind what looks like a chamber pot. There's a small collection of historic room keys, items of silverware, letters from guests including former Irish Taoiseach, Charles J Haughey (when he signed off, in 1952, the future Taoiseach was a young accountant with Haughey, Boland & Guiney) and a top hat. Menus feature, too – at one dinner in 1921, guests were offered a choice of 'Clear Cockie Leckie Soup' or 'Thick Ox-Tail Soup', for example. After

enjoying the hotel's hospitality, not everybody went gently into the good night, however. A letter from the South African Rugby Tour of 1952 refers to a cheque for £716 enclosed 'for damages of furniture incurred during the visit of the above Team to your hotel.' Given what the Springboks do to opposing teams, one can only imagine what they did to the opulent interiors and tasteful furniture of this 19th-century establishment.

A small step is all it takes to pass from the inner sanctum of the hotel into this little glass time capsule. And all for the price of a cocktail …

BEN DUNNE'S BULLETS

Thank God I am free ...

Little Museum of Dublin, 15 St Stephen's Green, Dublin 2
01 661-1000
littlemuseum.ie
Daily 10am–5pm
Luas, St Stephen's Green (Green Line); Pearse/Tara Street DART stations
(10–15-min. walk); Dublin Buses stopping nearby include 7b, 11, 116, 118, 14,
142, 145, 15 and 46a

Payments to politicians, whizz business deals, cocaine … Ben Dunne's life has had more ups and downs than a yo-yo in a lift. But surely nothing in the straight-talking entrepreneur's chequered career could compare with the events of 16 October 1981.

On that day, Dunne was on his way to open a new Dunnes Stores in Northern Ireland when he was seized by four masked gunmen and held prisoner for several days. The Irish Republican army (IRA) demanded a ransom, which it has been alleged was paid to secure his release. The 34-year-old was eventually freed after television appeals and several meetings with the kidnappers by Fr Dermot McCarthy. Police on both sides of the Irish border sealed off escape routes in the area before Dunne was found outside a church on the border at Cullyhanna, Co. Armagh. 'He was dishevelled, bearded and seemed to be quite roughed over, although not injured in any way,' a Belfast reporter told the *Herald Tribune* at the time. 'All he could say was 'Thank God I am free. You don't know how glad I am.''

Before his release, on 22 October, two of Dunne's abductors handed him a couple of bullets, telling him that they could have been used on him and Fr McCarthy if the police had closed in. Afterwards, Dunne had the bullets mounted on a piece of stone from the Armagh cemetery where he had been held captive. They have since been donated to the Little Museum of Dublin, where you'll find them in a locked cabinet alongside a smorgasbord of other quirky artefacts from the city's 20th-century history – from rooms dedicated to U2 to a chunky old bus ticket machine.

Close by to Ben Dunne's bullets, look out for a facsimile of James Joyce's death mask. Joyce was 58 when he died in a Zurich hospital, following surgery for a perforated ulcer. The Irish government declined Nora Joyce's offer to permit the repatriation of his remains (Nora hit back by leaving his *Finnegans Wake* papers to the British Museum). Although you'll find another death mask at the Joyce Centre on Eccles Street, the author himself is buried in a grave in Fluntern Cemetery in Zurich.

HAUGHEY'S HONEY POT

A little something to keep them sweet

Little Museum of Dublin, 15 St Stephen's Green, Dublin 2
01 661-1000
littlemuseum.ie
Daily 10am–5pm
Luas, St Stephen's Green (Green Line); Pearse/Tara Street DART stations
(10–15-min. walk); Dublin Buses stopping nearby include 7b, 11, 116, 118, 14,
142, 145, 15 and 46a

Charles J. Haughey (1925–2006) was the Machiavellian prince of Irish politics. A Taoiseach (prime minister), minister, Fianna Fáil leader, republican, sailor, man-about-town, spendthrift, bon vivant, phone-tapper, Charvet shirt-wearer, patron of the arts and brass-balled hypocrite who told Ireland it was living 'way beyond [its] means' while himself enjoying a flash lifestyle way beyond his political salary – here was a personality as divisive as it was dominant over several decades in Irish politics.

'A consummate vote-getter, it was often said that he came from every county in Ireland,' as we are told (he was actually born in Castlebar). 'But he made his home in Dublin.'

Millions of words have been written, and no small number of portraits painted, of a man who would have been a shoe-in as Ireland's most controversial 20th-century politician until the economic ground fell from beneath Irish feet in recent years. As is often the case with larger-than-life public figures, however, it's not the big books and TV series that get to the essence of C. J. Haughey. In many cases, it's the smaller things – such as this inconspicuous-looking jar of Abbeville honey, mounted in a glass case in the Little Museum of Dublin. Few people know that Haughey was an avid bee-keeper, collecting honey from the hives at Abbeville, his Georgian mansion in Kinsealy, Co. Dublin. Fewer still are aware that he made a habit of gifting that honey to family and friends in jars such as the one on display … 'to keep them sweet'. Such a tiny jar, and yet it says so much.

The artefact – if you could call it that – was presented to the museum by Seán Haughey, son of the former Taoiseach, and it hangs in the middle of a wall jam-packed with Dublin lore. Other political items that catch the eye are Mary Robinson's poster from the 1990 presidential elections, a gift box from former Dublin Lord Mayor Alfie Byrne and Bertie Ahern's first election flyer from 1977. But few leave such a strong impression as the Haughey-related artefacts. As well as the honeypot, they include a monochrome portrait by Colman Doyle, and a painting that hung above Haughey's desk in Kinsealy for almost 40 years: 'Think Big,' it exhorts. Whatever else you think about the man, he certainly did that.

GAIETY THEATRE HAND PRINTS

Stars in the sidewalk

South King Street, off Grafton Street, Dublin 2
01 679-5622
gaietytheatre.ie
Tara Street DART station (10–15-min. walk); Luas, St Stephen's Green
(Green Line); Dublin Bus stops 790, 791 and 5034 are nearby on St Stephen's
Green and Dawson Street

Most visitors to the Gaiety are looking at the stars, so they could be forgiven for missing the array of plaques at their feet. Cast in bronze outside the theatre's Venetian façade, the collection of handprints is a who's-who of performers, including Luciano Pavarotti, Brian Friel, Peter Ustinov, Bernadette Greevy and John B. Keane … all of whom have graced the famous stage.

Like a souvenir-sized version of the collection at Grauman's Chinese Theatre in Hollywood, the handprints are a strangely endearing memento of the celebs they celebrate. The shiny, tactile prints almost invite you to stoop down, try your own paws for size and wriggle your fingers about in the cool, bronze indentations. It's far more personal than your standard stars in the sidewalk.

Pavarotti's prints are the *coup de grâce*. The Italian legend first sang here in 1963, during a Dublin Grand Opera Society performance of *Rigoletto*. He went on to become a star at Covent Garden, of course, but on South King Street, Pavarotti was 'just another good young kid on the block making his way,' as Opera Ireland archivist Paddy Brennan recalled after the tenor's death in 2007 – revealing that the great man joined a theatre troupe for a kickabout in Phoenix Park. 'He was a bloody great footballer,' Brennan told *The Irish Independent*. 'He was a big man … but as a young fellow, he had legs like a ballet dancer.' Pavarotti's hands were cast for posterity in 2001.

Since her own opening night on 27 November 1871, the Grand Old Lady has been one of Dublin's best-known and most beautiful theatre spaces. A populist programme of opera, ballet, dance, drama, pantos and musicals has been taken to heart by Dubliners, providing a playful complement to the more literary fare of the Gate and Abbey theatres. The handprints of Irish stars like Maureen Potter, Twink, Niall Toibín, Ronnie Drew, Milo O'Shea, Des Keogh and Rosaleen Linehan take pride of place on the pavement outside, but even international stars realise the generosity of the tribute.

'Well, I'm immortal,' as Rupert Everett said, leaving his handprints after *The Judas Kiss* in 2012. 'Everyday it rains on Dublin, I'll be able to think about it raining onto my little hands …'

ERIN & LUGH

Art Deco Dublin

Dept of Jobs, Enterprise & Innovation, 23 Kildare Street, Dublin 2
Pearse Street DART station (5–10-min. walk); Luas, St Stephen's Green
(Green Line; 10-min. walk); Dublin Bus stops 746, 747 and 4350 are located
on Kildare Street

Dublin, it's fair to say, is not known for its Art Deco treasures. But here's a humdinger: 'The most distinguished Government office building to be commissioned after the establishment of the Free State,' as Christine Casey describes it in *Dublin* (Yale University Press, 2005).

Completed in 1942 to a design by J. R. Barrett, the steel-framed building, which originally housed the Department of Industry and Commerce, somehow manages to combine dramatic bas-reliefs, a five-storey window, domineering keystones, weighty bronze gates and a ministerial balcony without completely dominating its Georgian neighbours. The limestone reliefs are by Gabriel Hayes, who designed Ireland's old 1p and 2p coins, and they bring a touch of Soviet propaganda to the fledgling Irish state – featuring stoic men in profile, working hard with hammers, wrenches, wheels and shovels as they cobble, mill, craft and manufacture high up above the passers-by. The most impressive six-pack belongs to Lugh, who appears to be tossing planes from a lintel above the Kildare Street entrance. His angular nose has been chipped, though so strappingly is the Celtic god of light portrayed, you'd doubt he even noticed. Overlooking all of this, atop the five-storey window with its Art Deco glazing, is Erin – the female embodiment of Ireland and a stern-faced woman on a mission. Along with the keystone depicting Brendan the Navigator around the corner, she was carved in situ.

Sadly, members of the public are not allowed inside today's Department of Jobs, Enterprise and Innovation. But you can rest easy in the knowledge that the minister of the day works in a walnut-panelled office with marble chimneypieces. This was the first Irish government building specifically designed for its purpose, and for all the unintentional comedy value, its Art Deco chevrons, zigzags and receding planes make a beautifully austere impression.

FREEMASON'S HALL

The HQ of freemasonry in Ireland

17 Molesworth Street, Dublin 2
01 676-1337; – freemason.ie
Monday–Friday 9am–5pm
Guided tours Monday–Friday 3pm (June, July & August). Otherwise by appointment
Pearse Street DART station (10-min. walk); Luas, St Stephen's Green (Green Line; 5–10-min. walk); Dublin Bus stops 792, 5034 and others are on Dawson Street

Irish freemasonry has a long and proud tradition. There's evidence of freemasons in the country as long as 500 years ago – and its Grand Lodge, established in 1725, is the second oldest in the world (the Grand Lodge of England was founded in 1717).

Freemason's Hall itself dates from the late 1860s and, as you'd expect from the HQ of Irish freemasonry, everything about the building is steeped in ceremony, symbol and exactitude. From dramatic set pieces like the Grand Lodge Room to the furtive squares and compasses hiding in door knockers, seatbacks and lapel pins, every centimetre of Edward Holmes' Victorian design reflects its masonic purpose. Despite the secret society stereotypes, tours are surprisingly open – taking in the Prince Masons' Room, the Egyptian-themed Hand Chapter Room, the Knights Templar Preceptory Room, a ground-floor museum and the undisputed highlight: the Grand Lodge Room. This is a dizzying piece of theatre, with velvet thrones surrounded by heavy drapes, studded leather benches and gilt-framed portraits of bigwig freemasons like Albert, Prince of Wales, and Augustus Fitzgerald, the Third Duke of Leinster. The black-and-white squared carpet is slightly disorienting, piling on the sense of drama as you access an esoteric organisation's inner sanctum.

Lodges from all over Ireland meet at Freemasons' Hall, but the best thing about the tour is the openness of the guides, who'll happily debunk any theories regarding the Illuminati, human lizards or fake moon landings. Arcane rituals are central, of course ('They're what sets us apart from a golf club') and it's true that there are secret handshakes, or 'grips', though membership is open to all men who believe in a Supreme Being.

Despite the stuffiness, membership is enjoying a boom in Ireland. Our guide attributed this partly to the Dan Brown phenomenon, but intrigue, theatre and ritual play their part too. 'It's boy scouts for big boys,' as he put it. 'And we've got nothing to hide.'

COLLECTION OF MEDICAL INSTRUMENTS

Weird and wonderful

Royal College of Physicians, 6 Kildare Street, Dublin 2
01 669-8801; rcpi.ie
By appointment
Admission: free
Pearse Street DART station (5–10-min. walk); Luas, St Stephen's Green
(Green Line; 10-min. walk); Dublin Bus stops 746, 747 and 4350 are nearby
on Kildare Street

The Royal College of Physicians of Ireland (RCPI) dates back to 1654, when Dr John Stearne founded his Fraternity of Physicians of Trinity Hall. A Royal Charter followed from King Charles II in 1667 and the college has gone on to amass probably Ireland's finest medical library.

Books aren't the only artefacts in its heritage collection, however. In the basement of this grand building on Kildare Street, you'll also find a weird and wonderful stash of medical instruments. Displayed behind glass, there's a mahogany medical case that once belonged to William Robert Kerans (1836–1914), an army surgeon who saw action in China during the Taiping Rebellion of 1860 and Egypt during the Urabi Revolt of 1882. There are obstetrical instruments dating from the 1700s, with one accompanying note describing a ghastly device designed 'to perforate the head of an infant, in order to lessen the size of it, by evacuating part of the brain'. There's a brass and ivory enema kit that slots into a discreet wooden case to avoid embarrassment (bound in leather to resemble a book, it even has the title *Morning Exercise* on the spine). There's a homeopathic guide from Leath & Ross, the first manufacturers of such medicines in Britain, and a facsimile notice from the National Association for the Prevention of Tuberculosis, warning the public: 'Do not spit!'

No. 6 Kildare Street itself was designed by William Murray, and constructed after a fire destroyed the original Kildare Street Club premises in 1860. It was completed in 1864, a year behind schedule – look closely and you'll find '1863' set into plasterwork, stained glass and other features throughout the interiors. Visitors are in for a treat, with a grand series of restored Victorian rooms stretching deep beyond the façade. They culminate in Corrigan Hall, a converted racquet hall whose high wooden ceiling was erected without nails.

NAPOLEON'S TOOTHBRUSH

The emperor and the Irishman

Royal College of Physicians of Ireland, 6 Kildare Street, Dublin 2
01 669-8801; rcpi.ie
By appointment
Admission: free
Pearse Street DART station (5–10-min. walk); Luas, St Stephen's Green
(Green Line; 10-min. walk); Dublin Bus stops 746, 747 and 4350 are nearby
on Kildare Street

Napoleon is known all over the world. Barry Edward O'Meara, not so much. Still, the Irish physician's close friendship with the French emperor was such that Napoleon not only trusted him to take notes for a posthumous diary, but gifted him some extraordinary personal effects – including his toothbrush and a pair of personalised snuffboxes.

The items, along with a small lancet used by O'Meara to bleed Napoleon, are found in a modest display case in a hallway of the Royal College of Physicians (RCPI) on Kildare Street. They date back to Napoleon's time on St Helena, where he was imprisoned after his surrender at the Battle of Waterloo in 1815. O'Meara, an army doctor who hailed from Dublin, was senior surgeon on the HMS *Bellerophon*, and Napoleon requested his presence on the island as his personal physician. During their time on St Helena, the emperor and the Irishman became close friends, with Napoleon encouraging O'Meara to keep a diary ('Doctor, it will make you a fortune, but please do not publish until I am dead,' he said). When O'Meara was dismissed from the island in 1818, he told the Admiralty that Napoleon needed to be brought to England for proper treatment – a gesture that saw him dismissed from the navy, lose his pension and struck from the medical register. Not one to let a situation get the better of him, O'Meara responded by establishing himself as a dentist, displaying Napoleon's wisdom tooth in his shop window. When the emperor died in 1821, his prediction came to pass: O'Meara published a diary based on his notes, and it won him fame and fortune.

O'Meara's mementos were dispersed after his death, but reunited by another Irish surgeon, Sir Frederick Conway Dwyer (1860–1935). When Conway Dwyer died, they were presented to the RCPI, where further evidence of Napoleon's personality cult can be found lodged between the antlers of a tiny wooden deer head. The cube of wood is said to be a piece of the emperor's coffin, dating from 1841 when his body was exhumed from St Helena.

SINÉAD O'CONNOR'S 'NO SECOND TROY'

Beauty like a tightened bow …

The National Library, 2/3 Kildare Street, Dublin 2
01 603-0200
nli.ie/yeats
Main Library exhibitions: Monday, Thursday & Friday, 9.30am–5pm;
Tuesday–Wednesday, 9:30am–7pm; Saturday–Sunday, 9.30am–5pm
Admission: free
Pearse Street DART station (5–10-min. walk); Luas, St Stephen's Green
(Green Line; 10-min. walk); Dublin Bus stops 746, 747 and 4350 are located
nearby on Kildare Street

The National Library's Yeats exhibition offers an award-winning insight into the life and work of Ireland's most famous poet – both through notebooks, manuscripts and artefacts donated by his late wife and son, and a series of audio-visual enclaves featuring snippets of sound and film.

Best of all are the inspired matches of modern voices with classic poems – read aloud and played on a loop in a hushed, octagonal space accompanied by images on screen (lake isles, Sligo scenery, Maud Gonne and the like). Seamus Heaney and Theo Dorgan are among them, but the big surprise, and absolute highlight, is Sinéad O'Connor's reading of 'No Second Troy'.

W. B. Yeats's short, taut poem poses a series of rhetorical questions about his muse ('Why should I blame her that she filled my days with misery …') and is almost universally known by people schooled in Ireland thanks to its inclusion in the Leaving Certificate anthology, *Soundings* (Gill & MacMillan, 1969). O'Connor's voice blows its cobwebs away with every syllable. Freshly enunciating the familiar lines, her tone fluctuates from a hardness underlined by her Dublin accent, to a syrupy sensuality, to a wounded vulnerability heightened by the listener's intimate knowledge of her own controversial life. It's an inspired pairing of voice and verse, breathing new life into old words:

> *What could have made her peaceful with a mind*
> *That nobleness made simple as a fire,*
> *With beauty like a tightened bow …*

Dating from 1890, the National Library's architectural highlight is undoubtedly its main reading room (visitors can peek, as long as they don't disturb diligent readers beneath the dome).

But there are hidden gems to be found elsewhere in the building too. Look out for the owl symbolising Wisdom in the Front Hall's mosaic floor, or the wooden fire surrounds carved by Carlo Cambi of Siena. Even the toilets are worth a visit (check out the armchairs) in a building with the lofty aim of collecting, preserving and promoting 'the larger universe of recorded knowledge'. Phew.

THE ANIMAL CARVINGS OF KILDARE STREET

Monkey business

The National Library, 2/3 Kildare Street, Dublin 2
01 603-0200
nli.ie
Admission: free
Pearse Street DART station (5–10-min. walk); Dublin Bus stops 746, 747 and 4350 stop nearby on Kildare Street

'A generation of men is like a generation of leaves.' So runs a quote by Homer inside the National Library's exhibition space on Kildare Street. Judging by the carvings at the base of the columns outside its sash windows, however, not everyone takes such a poetic view.

In a former life, this wing of the library served as the Kildare Street Club – a gentleman's clique attended by the upper crust of Dublin society. Strangely, however, the carvings anchoring its columns depict birds of prey, a dog chasing a rabbit and, best of all, three squawking monkeys playing billiards. What gives? The craftsmen responsible for the carvings were the O'Shea brothers, Cork-born stonemasons who rose to fame in 19th-century Dublin (they also worked on Trinity College's Museum building). Members of the Kildare Club would no doubt have enjoyed billiards, among other pursuits – leading one to wonder whether the O'Sheas were conspiring with them in a joke. Or perhaps they were making a subtle comment on an evolving British Empire? Similar monkeys carved by the brothers were removed from the Oxford Museum during the fallout following the publication of Darwin's *On the Origin of Species*, as Anto Howard writes in *Slow Dublin* (Hardie Grant Publishing, 2010). At the time, outraged critics refused to believe that man could have descended from the primates.

Most tempting is the theory suggesting that the animals are a sly dig at the privileged members who would have swanned about inside. The Kildare Club 'represents all that is respectable', George Moore once said. 'That is to say, those who are gifted with that oyster-like capacity for understanding … that they should continue to get fat in the bed in which they were born.'

Monkey business, in other words.

MCCLINTOCK'S POLAR BEAR

The bear with the bullet hole ...

Natural History Museum, Merrion Square, Dublin 2
museum.ie
Tuesday to Saturday 10am–5pm, Sunday to Monday 1pm–5pm
Admission: free
Pearse Street DART station (5 to 10-min walk); Luas, St Stephen's Green
(Green Line; 10 to 15-min walk); Dublin Bus stop 2811 is right outside the
museum

It almost looks like a third eye. But the black hole in the forehead of the Natural History Museum's polar bear was carved by a bullet. It's a pretty direct reminder of the fact that the stuffed animals on display here were once ... well, animals. Not to mention the fact that collecting them left a legacy of destruction as much as education.

The museum's polar bear was shot in the late 1850s during an expedition in the Canadian Arctic led by Francis Leopold McClintock (1819–1907). Hailing from Drogheda, County Louth, McClintock was a veteran of Arctic travel, and his mission was to track down the remains of an ill-fated exhibition led years previously by Sir John Franklin. Franklin disappeared while attempting to chart a section of the Northwest Passage in 1847 – losing his entire crew of 130 to starvation, hypothermia and disease after their icebound ships were abandoned in the inhospitable climate. McClintock's team found several bodies, in addition to written records and artefacts from Franklin's party, and brought back the skin of a polar bear among his souvenirs – the one displayed in the museum. Look for the musk ox and calf on the first floor nearby – these also come courtesy of McClintock, whose team shot and ate them as they trekked across the Canadian Arctic.

Beginning with a collection bought by the Royal Dublin Society in 1792, the Natural History Museum's teeming cases of minerals, animals, fish and insects quickly expanded thanks to regular donations, and moved to the current building in 1857 – around 10,000 items have been on display. It's a museum that feels dated and fusty, like it should be displayed in a Victorian cabinet of its own, but one that holds a special place in the hearts of Dubliners – and a large-scale refurbishment is currently underway (some parts of the building may be off-limits). It's as enjoyable for its Victoriana as its wildlife, and its education team has come up with some super programmes for families and children, too.

McClintock's polar bear isn't the only celebrity on show – other animals came thanks to such famous explorers as Thomas Heazle, whose statue can be seen at the front of the building, and luminaries like King George V, who donated the Bengal Tiger in 1913.

PRINCE ALBERT MEMORIAL

Dublin's only royal monument

Leinster Lawn, Dublin 2
Pearse Street DART station (5-min. walk); Luas, St Stephen's Green (Green Line; 10–15-min. walk); Dublin Bus stops 2810 and 2811 are on Merrion Square West

t's a puzzle fit for a pub quiz. Where is Dublin's only surviving royal monument?

The answer lies hidden away in the lawn of Leinster House, where a black-bronze statue of Prince Albert stands with its back to the Natural History Museum.

The monument has done well to survive at all. In 1929, after all, Dublin's statue of William III in College Green was blown up. Another royal likeness, that of Queen Victoria, was removed from its pitch outside Leinster House in 1947 and stored for decades before eventually making its way to a second life in Sydney in the 1980s. No other imperial monuments remain on public display in the capital – which makes this one all the more remarkable.

The prospect of a memorial to Prince Albert was first mooted in the early 1860s, when the Dublin Prince Albert Statue Committee sought to erect their tribute in Stephen's Green, which they hoped would open to the public as 'Albert Park'. After a parliamentary bill knocked that on the head, the ancient city junction of College Green was proposed, and in turn slammed by Irish nationalists. 'In the coming days of revolutionary conflict, if an Albert statue should cumber the ground in College Green, it could easily be pulled down, and the bronze would come in handy for the casting of bullets or cannon for the patriot army,' as one Fenian told T. D. O'Sullivan, author of *Troubled Times in Irish Politics* (1905). Today's statue of Henry Grattan took pride of place in that particular location in 1875.

In the end, Prince Albert was sculpted by John Henry Foley – the man behind both the Albert Memorial in London's Kensington Gardens and the Daniel O'Connell Monument on O'Connell Street – and placed on Leinster Lawn in 1872. Queen Victoria was not impressed, as James Loughlin writes in *The British Monarchy and Ireland, 1800 to the Present* (2011): 'Victoria, obsessed with grief over Albert's death throughout the 1860s, perceived an insult she would not forget.' The sentiment went both ways, however. After repeated threats by Republicans, the statue was moved from a central spot on the lawn to its current protected site in 1924.

PORTRAIT OF DOÑA ANTONIA ZÁRATE

Silent witness to an art heist

National Gallery, Merrion Square, Dublin 1
01 661-5133 – nationalgallery.ie
Monday 11am–5.30pm; Tuesday & Wednesday 9.15am–5.30pm;
Thursday 9.15am–8.30pm; Friday & Saturday 9.15am–5.30pm;
Sunday 11am–5.30pm
Admission: free
Pearse Street DART station (5-min. walk); Dublin Bus routes 4, 5, 6, 7, 7a,
39/a, 46a, 13a, 44, 48a and 45 all stop nearby on Merrion Square

She looks a little vacant, sitting there. Curly locks, a black gown and lace mantilla contrast sumptuously with her lemon-yellow damask settee. But however you might describe this sultry Spanish actress, Doña Antonia Zárate seems a million miles from skulduggery of any sort.

That wasn't the case on the night of 26 April 1974. 'That painting means a great deal to me for two reasons,' as Lady Clementine Beit later explained. 'Alfred was standing beneath it when he proposed to me, and we were tied up under it during the Dugdale raid.'

Sir Alfred and Lady Clementine Beit owned the Goya. In 1952 this dashing couple had bought Russborough House, a magnificent Palladian mansion near Blessington, Co. Wicklow, specifically to house their art collection. Mick Jagger, Fred Astaire and Jackie Kennedy were just some of the guests who enjoyed the paintings over the years... but there were uninvited guests too. Russborough was raided several times during the Beits' tenure – including a heist by IRA members led by rogue British heiress, Rose Dugdale, in 1974. On that occasion, Sir Alfred and Lady Beit were tied up in their salon and pistol whipped as their *Portrait of Doña Antonia Zárate* was cut from its frame with a screwdriver. Luckily, the Beits survived and their paintings were recovered. In 1987 the couple donated a large portion of their collection to the National Gallery, in what was described as 'one of the most magnificent [donations] ever received by any museum, anywhere'. Goya's portrait was included, despite being missing at the time – it was stolen once again, along with a tranche of other paintings, in a 1986 raid by Dublin gangster Martin 'The General' Cahill. It was only after a police sting in Antwerp several years later that Doña Antonia Zárate finally made it to the gallery walls.

'This is one of Goya's most striking female portraits,' the gallery blub reports. Though few – if any – of the visitors shuffling past know anything of her 20th-century adventures.

The Beit Collection isn't the National Gallery's only donation of international significance. In 1900 its governors and guardians accepted from Henry Vaughan a bequest of 31 watercolours by J. M. W. Turner ... on the condition that they be shown only during the month of January.

SWENY'S CHEMIST

33

The literary pharmacy

1 Lincoln Place, Dublin 2
087 713-2157 (11am-5pm); 085 814-6713 (after 5pm)
sweny.ie
Monday–Friday 11am–6pm
Admission: free
Pearse Street DART station (5-min. walk); Dublin Bus stops 408 and 2809
are nearby on Clare Street and Westland Row, respectively

James Joyce was nothing if not fastidious. Were Dublin to be destroyed, the author is said to have believed it could be rebuilt from the pages of *Ulysses*. And so much has changed since the novel was first published in 1922 that Joyce's masterpiece is indeed starting to look as much like a record of the Edwardian cityscape as a work of fiction. Nelson's Pillar, the red light district of Monto, 7 Eccles Street and Barney Kiernan's pub are just a handful of its locations that have disappeared.

Sweny's Chemist is a notable survivor. Dating from 1847, this little pharmacy crops up in *Ulysses* when Leopold Bloom calls to collect a prescription for his wife, Molly. 'He waited by the counter, inhaling the keen reek of drugs, the dusty dry smell of sponges and loofahs. Lot of time taken up telling your aches and pains,' he thinks. 'Chemists rarely move. Their green and gold beacon jars too heavy to stir ... Smell almost cure you like the dentist's doorbell.' Although his prescription is not ready, Bloom does leave with a bar of lemon soap – the sweet scent of which has proved irresistible. In 1904 Joyce himself is known to have visited the same premises to consult with pharmacist Frederick William Sweny, and he drew heavily from memory in recreating the fusty interior.

Sweny's shut up shop in 2009, and for a time looked like it too might join the city's growing list of lost literary locations. Fortunately, however, a group of Joycean enthusiasts stepped in, negotiated a rent, staffed it on a voluntary basis and have managed to keep it going by selling books, postcards, curios – and yes, bars of lemon soap. Regular readings of *Dubliners*, *Ulysses* and *Finnegans Wake* are held, but what's most remarkable is that the interior remains almost exactly as Bloom and Joyce would have experienced it over a century ago. Rich mahogany counters take up most of the floor space. Blue bottles and bric-a-brac gather dust on dark shelves. In the old dispensary drawers, unclaimed prescriptions bound in brown paper and string date back to 1903.

Despite the city-centre traffic, bustling footsteps and whining alarms outside, you get completely caught up in the words and the world of the books. For a moment, the city is rebuilt.

FINN'S HOTEL SIGN

34

A Memory of the Artist as a Young Man ...

Leinster Street South, Dublin 2
Pearse Street DART station (5-min. walk); Luas, St Stephen's Green (Green Line; 10- min. walk); Dublin Bus stops 404, 405, 406 and 494 are a short walk away

Back in the early 1990s, a Dublin scholar discovered the literary equivalent of Tutankhamun's tomb. Or so he thought. Danis Rose had been working on a critical edition of *Finnegans Wake* when he claimed to have unearthed an unknown work by James Joyce … a series of sketches written between *Ulysses* and *Finnegans Wake* and which he believed were to be titled 'Finn's Hotel'.

Although other scholars had known about the sketches, most had held that they were early drafts of *Finnegans Wake*. Based on his reading of freshly released letters, however, Rose argued otherwise. 'There can be no doubt that 'Finn's Hotel' should be viewed apart from any other work, as a place that Joyce went to after *Ulysses* and from whence he came to *Finnegans Wake*,' he told the *New York Times*. Objections by the Joyce Estate meant that the stories were never published in their own right, however, and the controversial scholar's theory failed to launch.

Whatever the truth about the sketches, the real Finn's Hotel did play a significant role in Joyce's life. Overlooking Trinity College on Leinster Street South, Finn's harboured a small warren of rooms that sprawled over two redbrick houses, and though it no longer exists today, the hotel's sign is still painted on the terrace's gable end. Joycean enthusiasts fondly remember Finn's because it was here that the author first set eyes on Nora Barnacle, the love of his life. Barnacle worked as a chambermaid at Finn's and later stopped to talk to the 22-year-old on Nassau Street. Their first date took place on 16 June 1904 – the day on which *Ulysses* is set and Bloomsday celebrated. The sign was carefully restored during a recent refurbishment of the buildings.

In subsequent years, Joyce would revisit the hotel – described by his biographer, Richard Ellmann, as 'a slightly exalted boarding house' – when he returned to Dublin as part of a business venture aiming to establish the Volta cinema on Mary Street. He asked a waitress there to show him Nora's room and rapturously recounted the experience in a letter to his sweetheart. Like Three Kings kneeling before the manger, he gushed, 'I had brought my errors and follies and sins and wondering and longing to lay them at the little bed in which a young girl had dreamed of me.'

A brilliant and bizarre little collection

Zoology Dept., Trinity College, Dublin 2
01 896-1366
tcd.ie/zoology
Open summer only or by appointment
Admission: free
Pearse Street DART station (5-min. walk); Luas, St Stephen's Green (Green Line; 10–15-min. walk); Dublin Bus stops 405, 494, 2809 and others are nearby

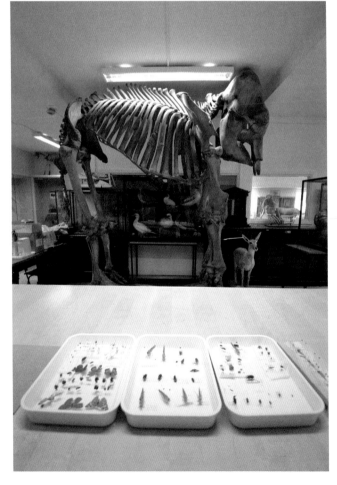

It's a museum that should be in a museum. Squirrelled away amid the offices, labs and lecture rooms of Trinity College's Zoology Department, this brilliant and bizarre little collection contains everything from a stuffed auk to the skeleton of an elephant. It's like someone kidnapped a corner of the Natural History Museum ... without telling a soul.

Little known though it is, the Zoological Museum has a long tradition. A collection begun over 250 years ago was once one of the most important teaching museums of its day – prompting a purpose-built building in 1876. Today's visit is confined to a small corner of the first floor, but at least the museum's short-term future looks bright, with a refurbishment recently achieved thanks to generous donations and an enthusiastic curator.

Browsing the display cases, you'll find spectacular creatures in various states of preservation: insects on pins, fish in formaldehyde, specimens in jars, a stuffed Tanzanian Wolf rivalling any of the smaller mounts in the National Museum's 'Dead Zoo' up the road. The Great Auk is the only species with the 'dubious privilege' of a precisely known point of extinction, visitors learn: on 22 June 1844 the last remaining pair was strangled and cast into a boat off the south-west tip of Iceland. Warming to the theme, Trinity's specimen was the last of its kind to have been recorded in Ireland (found swimming off the Co. Waterford coast in 1834). The Board of the university even granted a 'great auk pension' of £50 a year to the ornithologist who donated it.

Across the room stands the skeleton of 'Prince Tom', an Asian elephant donated to Dublin Zoo by the Duke of Edinburgh. Upon its death in 1882, the animal was transferred on a float to Trinity College, where it was enthusiastically dissected 'with the aid of shears, ropes and pulleys', in the words of Catherine De Courcy, author of *Dublin Zoo: An Illustrated History* (Collins Press, 2009).

Don't miss the stuffed Great Indian Rhino, either – a display panel informs us that the animal was 'confused in the past with the mythical unicorn'.

MUSEUM BUILDING

Trinity's rock stars ...

Trinity College, Dublin 2
tcd.ie/geology
Monday–Friday 9am–5pm
Pearse Street DART station (5-min walk); Luas, St Stephen's Green (Green Line; 10 to 15-min walk); Dublin Bus stops 405, 494, 2809 and others are nearby

Trinity's Museum Building, home to its Geology Department, was inspired by the Venetian-Byzantine style of architecture. Built between 1853 and 1857 to designs by Thomas Deane and Benjamin Woodward, its ground-floor hall is a beautiful piece of work, and can be visited by the public on weekdays.

Faced with Caen limestone, the inner walls here feature carvings by the O'Shea brothers (who gathered fresh flowers as their models), columns and balustrades containing examples of Irish marbles and Cornish serpentine, and an arching dome constructed from blue, red and yellow enamelled bricks. Right inside the door, you can't miss the male and female Irish elk (Megaloceros giganteus) skeletons, but continue nosing about and you'll also find several additional displays – ranging from fossilised Chirotherium footprints to an illustration of life's evolution on Earth.

All are from the university's Geological Museum – a collection of over 100,000 specimens ranging from meteorites to fossils, dinosaur bones and mineral collections drawn from the three rock types: igneous, metamorphic and sedimentary. The collection dates from 1777, and indeed, the Museum Building was purpose-built in the 1850s to house it and the university's growing stock of geological, botanical, ethnographical, zoological, engineering and other wonders. As the campus evolved, however, the collections were dispersed, and locating them is today something of a treasure hunt.

In recent times, the Geology Museum lurked upstairs. To see its rock stars, visitors followed a sequence of signs up a series of shrinking stairways before eventually arriving in a stuffy room lined with old display cases. Here, you could pore over everything from corals to cephalopods and even a few glittering handfuls of industrial diamonds under the watchful eyes of a red deer skeleton and a wooden model of a pterodactyl. Today, the museum has been closed (it's open by appointment via the department's website), though displays 'on topical aspects of Geology' continue to be exhibited in the hall cabinets.

CHALLONER'S CORNER

Dublin's smallest cemetery

Front Square, Trinity College, Dublin 2
01 896-1000
tcd.ie/visitors
Tara Street & Pearse Street DART stations (5-min. walk); Luas, St Stephen's
Green (Green Line) and Abbey Street (Red Line) (5-min. walk)

Trinity College isn't short on ceremony. Or celebrated alumni, for that matter. Which is one reason it's surprising to find this tiny cemetery squirrelled away in such an inconspicuous nook off Front Square. Set at waist-height above an ATM in a passageway between the College Chapel and Dining Hall, it's almost as if it was hidden on purpose.

That's part of its charm, of course. Said to be Dublin's smallest cemetery, Challoner's Corner takes its name from Luke Challoner, one of Trinity's first Fellows and a leading light in the years following its establishment in 1592. Challoner's private book collection formed the basis of the Old Library here, and he developed it further over the course of several purchasing trips to London with James Usher, a future Archbishop of Armagh. A monument from his tomb can be seen in the little enclosure, though you'll have less luck with the faded inscription. Originally housed in the old College Chapel, the monument was moved outdoors when the building was replaced in 1798 and the elements have taken their toll (there is said to have been an alabaster figure, but any trace of it has long since weathered away). A translation of Challoner's Latin epitaph, from *Fuller's Church History of Britain* (1665), reads:

> This tomb within it here contains,
> Of Chalnor the said remains;
> By whose prayer, and helping hand,
> This House erected here doth stand.

Among the other former Provosts and Fellows remembered here are John Sterne (1660–1745), who built the Printing House, and George Browne, whose death in 1699 was partly the result of an injury sustained during a college riot. Browne's is the overblown mural tablet flanked with Corinthian columns, though its lengthy Latin inscription makes no reference to his being struck by a brickbat while on his way to admonish some students …

Not that it's all ancient history. Select souls continue to have their epitaphs cast in stone at Challoner's Corner – hence the memorials to former Provosts William Arthur Watts, who died in 2010, and Francis Stewart Leland Lyons, who passed away in 1983. Despite its forgotten feel, the souvenir-sized cemetery has a quiet dignity – tidily kept as it is, and surrounded by leafy bushes, scholarly stone, and memorials almost close enough to touch. It's hard to believe the busy city centre junction of College Green is just footsteps away.

PLAQUE FOR FATHER PAT NOISE

The craic with the plaque

O'Connell Bridge, Dublin 2
Tara Street DART station (5-min. walk); Luas, Abbey Street (Red Line);
numerous Dublin Buses stop along O'Connell Street and the quays

THIS PLAQUE COMMEMORATES
Fr. PAT NOISE
ADVISOR TO PEADAR CLANCEY.
HE DIED UNDER SUSPICIOUS
CIRCUMSTANCES WHEN HIS
CARRIAGE PLUNGED INTO THE
LIFFEY ON AUGUST 10th 1919.

ERECTED BY
THE HSTI

Father Pat Noise was a priest who died under suspicious circumstances when his carriage plunged into the River Liffey on 10 August 1919.

Or was he? Certainly, the small bronze plaque embedded in the west side of O'Connell Bridge appears to commemorate a real man. But in fact, it's a hoax. Snugly designed to fit a space once occupied by a control box for the city's ill-fated Millennium Clock, the plaque was installed in broad daylight in 2004 and lay unnoticed by Dublin City Council for two years. 'It is certainly very unusual for this to happen,' Council representatives told the *Sunday Tribune*, which first brought it to their attention. After examining the unauthorised memorial, the Council stated that it would be removed.

Father Noise, whose profile features in relief on the plaque, is described as 'an advisor to Peadar Clancy' – a real-life Irish Republican who fought in the Easter Rising and was killed in Dublin Castle on Bloody Sunday (21 November 1920). It has been suggested that 'Pat Noise' is a play on the Latin for 'Our Father' (*Pater Noster*). Video footage later supplied by the hoaxers, which apparently shows them installing the plaque on this busy bridge, described it as a tribute to their father. The plaque states that it was 'erected by the HSTI' – a playfully rude anagram opening it up to all sorts of interpretation. Is the plaque a comment on Ireland's dubious tradition of spending public money on projects like the Millennium Clock, which was festooned with weeds within weeks of its installation? Is it a comment on Irish Republicanism, the Catholic Church, or a simple act of mischief that encapsulates the Irish love of a good giggle, an imaginative prank and pulling a fast one on the authorities?

It's a memorial to sheer persistence, too. After the Council removed the plaque in 2007, a replacement appeared within months. That, too, was threatened with removal, until a growing show of public support prompted a south-east area committee vote to retain it.

Critics decry a juvenile act of vandalism, but it remains in place today.

CON HOULIHAN'S 'SHRINE'

'He's loved by young and old …'

Mulligan's Pub, 2 Poolbeg Street,
Dublin 2
01 677-5582
mulligans.ie
Monday–Thursday noon–11.30pm, Friday & Saturday 11am–12.30pm,
Sunday 12.30pm–11pm
Tara Street DART station (2-min. walk); Luas, Abbey Street (Red Line;
5-min. walk); several Dublin Bus stops are nearby on Hawkins Street and
D'Olier Street

Thanks to its grubby elegance and blistering literary credentials, Mulligan's is one of the most hallowed drinking holes in Dublin. Push through the doors on Poolbeg Street, and all it takes is a magical little moment for your eyes to adjust, for dark spaces awash with worn-down counters, oily wallpaper, gas lamp fittings and cracked leather stools to emerge.

It feels like it has always been thus: when John Mulligan leased the premises in 1854; when James Joyce staged a back parlour arm wrestle in his short story, 'Counterparts'; when a young JFK sank a pint in 1945; when stars like Julia Roberts and Judy Garland pulled up a pew.

Famous as its visitors have been, it speaks volumes about the place that none of them are celebrated in cheesy memorials on the walls. None of them, that is, except Con Houlihan. He gets not only a photograph, but a veritable shrine.

Houlihan (1925–2012) was a sports writer who churned out such colourful, funny and transcendent work for the Irish Press Group – and later for Independent Newspapers – that he ranked in the public imagination alongside literary lights like Behan, Kavanagh and Flann O'Brien (indeed, all four are captured in pavement plaques outside another of Houlihan's favourite haunts, The Palace). The Kerryman was also a giant of the Dublin pub scene, and the mounted photograph here captures him at his 'office' with customary glass of brandy and milk in hand. Houlihan regularly composed his copy in Mulligan's, and even lodged cheques behind the bar. As a fellow sports journalist, Ian O'Riordan of *The Irish Times*, put it after Houlihan's death at 86: 'Even after a hard day's night he would – sometimes astonishingly – be at his desk before dawn to handwrite his column.'

'Con Houlihan is the greatest living sports journalist,' runs a quote from John B. Keane on the shrine – a hodgepodge of wood, brass and the odd typo that's all the more endearing for its gaudiness. 'When he entered the sporting scene, the cobwebs of bias and bigotry were blown away by the pure breath of his vision and honesty. I played rugby against him but drank porter with him. We were useful enough players but we excelled at the other …'

At the bottom, a poem by Brendan Kennelly concludes:

He's loved by young and old,
He's [sic] words are bright and true
Making the thoughtless think, The humourless laugh
Now that's a hard thing to do …

DIVING BELL

Dublin's Docklands belle

Sir John Rogerson's Quay, Dublin 2
Open 24/7
Admission: free
Pearse Street and Grand Canal Dock DART stations are both a 10–15-min.
walk away; Dublin Bus stops 7512, 7076 and 7077 are nearby

For years, it looked like it was destined for the scrapheap, but this big, brash and bright-orange chunk of metal on Sir John Rogerson's Quay turned out to be treasure rather than trash. Until its recent refurbishment, how many passers-by would have known that the unlikely looking device was, in fact, originally designed as a diving bell for dredging the Liffey channel?

Following a four-month restoration in 2015, the Diving Bell is now a visitor attraction. Pedestrians who once peered into its portholes can today step inside, absorbing its unlikely history through a series of interpretive panels. The bell dates back to 1860, they learn, when it was designed by the brilliantly named Bindon Blood Stoney (the former port engineer, memorialised in nearby Blood Stoney Street). At the time, Dublin Port was undergoing an expansion, with deep-water quays deemed necessary to facilitate the growing number of steam ships seeking to access the city. Instead of using traditional cofferdam techniques to construct the new docks, Stoney came up with the radical solution of laying prefabricated concrete slabs on a seabed and then flattening them by using a diving bell hung from a floating barge. The bell's 20-ft-square [1.86 sq. m] airlocked chamber and access shaft are now elevated, allowing visitors to step into the space where pods of men would have worked in shifts. If you think it's claustrophobic today, just imagine what it was like back then – a hot chamber, in which workers often suffered ear traumas in the compressed air (although there are no records of fatalities or serious mishaps).

Stoney's was a remarkable achievement – right down to the large-scale use of concrete, a technique in its infancy at the time (the deep-water quays built on his watch are still capable of receiving the largest ships entering the port). The bell itself was used right up to the 1950s, when shifts were at least alleviated by electric light and a telephone, according to Cormac F. Lowth, writing in *The International Journal of Diving History*. According to Lowth, 'One of the few perks of working in the diving bell was to find a few plump flatfish that had been left behind on the bottom when the water receded, for [the men's] supper.'

CHIMNEY PARK

A smokin' inner-city oasis

Off Grand Canal Square, Dublin 2
Pearse Street and Grand Canal Dock DART stations (both a 10–15-min. walk); Luas, Spencer Dock (Red Line: 10–15-min. walk); Dublin Bus stops 7512, 7076 and 7077 are nearby

Joined-up thinking can never be taken for granted in a city. Yet here, tucked away just a few steps from the evolving urban landscape of Grand Canal Square, is a sandy little space that looks and feels like it was designed by the people, for the people.

Chimney Park opened in 2009, just after the Celtic Tiger was snared in a merciless trap of recession. At the time, it was clear the South Docklands could no longer be the soaring city quarter that planners and developers had dreamed up in the noughties. Certain landmark buildings got in before the financiers pulled out, however – including The Marker, a five-star hotel designed by Manuel Aires Mateus, and the Bord Gáis Energy Theatre, an ambitious centrepiece realised in signature style by Daniel Libeskind. Concealed behind the former (and beside the latter) is where you'll find the modest little Chimney Park.

Revolving around a restored redbrick chimney on the former Dublin Gasworks site, this appears at first glance to be a casual space. But don't be fooled: a huge amount of consultation with stakeholders and local parties went into a design that shines in the detail. Closer inspection of the playground reveals unusual touches like mirrored walls and clever little grip-bricks inserted into the base of the chimney – transforming it into a climbing wall. Children from the local City Quay National School even created a special poem, 'Talking Chimney', which has been engraved into the park benches. All that remains is for people to find it …

Dublin's South Docklands are criss-crossed by some of the most evocative street names in the city. Look out for Blood Stoney Road, for example, named for the pioneering former port engineer, Bindon Blood Stoney. Nearby, Lazer Lane stems from 'Lazaretto', which recalls the former nearby quarantine stations for lepers and sailors.

Best of all, perhaps, is Misery Hill – apparently deriving its name from a time when corpses from the gallows at Baggot Street 'were strung up to rot as a warning to other troublemakers', as Turtle Bunbury writes in *Dublin Docklands – An Urban Voyage* (Montague, 2008).

DUBLIN CITY ARCHIVES

Nelson's head and Bang Bang's Colt 45

128–144 Pearse Street, Dublin 2
01 674-4999
dublincity.ie
By appointment, Wednesday–Thursday 10am–12.30pm and 2pm–4.30pm
Admission: free
Pearse Street DART station (5-min. walk); Dublin Bus stops 351 and 398 are
outside and opposite the library building, respectively

Dublin City Archives contain records stretching from 1171 to the late 20th century. A trove of City Council documents, court records, title deeds, maps, plans, electoral rolls, newspaper archives and church, land and emigration records all document the development of Dublin over the centuries. Anyone can visit, provided they bring the ID necessary to obtain a research card at the desk and abide by the rules – no photos, pens, food or phones.

It's not just paper records, either. A torch from the 2012 London Olympics is on display, and Nelson's head stands on a plinth in the corner of the reading room. Not his actual head, mind you – but that of the 13ft (4m) figure that came crashing to earth when the IRA blew up Nelson's Pillar on O'Connell Street in 1966. 'There was an almighty flash and a sound like a clap of thunder,' as a local taxi man, stopped at nearby traffic lights, recalls in a contemporary news story displayed alongside. 'I just had time to get out.' The head took a battering, but remains remarkably intact considering the height from which it fell – not to mention a previous, ill-fated attempt by UCD (University College Dublin) students to melt it in the 1950s. For all the effort to destroy him, Nelson still keeps his one good eye on the citizens in this room.

Another item in the archives – humbler, but just as engaging – is the Colt 45 once brandished by Thomas 'Bang Bang' Dudley (1906–89). Bang Bang 'shot' thousands of people around Dublin, but was never held to account for his crimes. The reason? His 'gun' was a church key. 'He used to shoot me with that every day,' says Leo Magee, a porter working at the archives and one of many Dubliners with fond memories of Dudley's cowboy antics in cinemas, trams and on streets throughout the city. 'With a final theatrical flourish, a victorious Bang Bang would then gallop off into the distance, slapping his rear end as if he were on a horse,' as Paul Drury recalled in a feature for the *Irish Daily Mail*.

'The whole city was mine,' Dudley told another paper, the *Evening Press*, in 1979. And scouring through the books and records here, it's hard not to feel the same way.

ARCHER'S GARAGE

The building that rose from the dead

Fenian Street, Dublin 1
Pearse Street DART station (5-min. walk); Dublin Buses 120, 27x, 4, 7 and 8
stop at bus stop 408 on nearby Merrion Square

Dublin is full of beautiful architecture. Like any big city, however, it is also blighted by hundreds (some might say thousands) of horrendous architectural crimes.

Think of the row of Georgian town houses demolished to make way for the ESB office block on Fitzwilliam Street. Ponder the loss of No. 7 Eccles Street, one of the most famous addresses in world literature. Consider the destruction of the former Theatre Royal in 1962 to make way for Hawkins House, the sickly-looking Department of Health HQ. Even the famed Wide Streets Commission razed much of the city's medieval fabric, stealthily creating arteries like modern-day Parliament Street, 'with workmen reportedly removing roofs from sleeping inhabitants', as Niall McCullough writes in *Dublin: An Urban History* (Lilliput, 2007).

For a short time following one weekend in June 1999, it looked as if Archer's Garage was to be the latest casualty of rampant development. An ambitious, art deco-inspired building that turned a nifty corner on Fenian Street, Archer's was the first building in Ireland to be constructed from reinforced concrete… not to mention fitted with funky fluorescent lighting. Designed by Arnold Francis Hendy and dating from the late 1940s, it sold and serviced Ford automobiles in its day, but by the late 1990s was the only remaining building on a site earmarked for a new apartment complex. Despite being Grade 1 listed, Archer's was destroyed by contractors working for a well-known Dublin developer while city watchdogs (and eagle-eyed citizens) were off-duty, enjoying a Bank Holiday weekend.

A public outcry duly ensued, with Dublin City Council ordering the developer to restore the garage or risk a hefty fine and/or imprisonment. Archer's quickly became a poster child for a reckless style of development in the city and an endemic slowness to recognise and adequately protect Dublin's 20th-century architecture. It took fully five years to finally be reinstated.

If you drive by the corner of Fenian and Sandwith Streets today, don't bother pulling into the garage for a can of oil (inviting though the forecourt, with its thick white supporting column, may seem). The chalk-white building now forms the entrance to an adjoining office block and is occupied by a bank. It's not a perfect replica of the original – whose merits Dublin wags would no doubt have disputed in the first place – but it is a testimony to one victory against cavalier developers.

For fans of architecture, Archer's will always be the building that rose from the dead.

JOKER'S CHAIR

All the rest is laughter …

Merrion Square Park, Dublin 2
dublincity.ie
December and January 10am–5pm; February and November 10am–5.30pm;
March and October 10am– 6.30pm; April and September 10am–8.30pm;
May and August 10am–9.30pm; June and July 10am–10pm
Pearse Street DART station (5-min walk); Dublin Bus stops 408, 494 and
2810 are close to Clare Street and the north-west entrance

Merrion Square dates from 1762, when its first townhouses were built. Though mainly housing offices today, in its heyday the Georgian square was one of Dublin's most fashionable addresses – and former residents included Oscar Wilde (who lived at No.1, across from which you'll find his coy sculpture by Danny Osborne), Daniel O'Connell (No.58) and W. B. Yeats (No.82). All would have held keys to what was then a private park.

In 1930 the Catholic Church bought the green space with the intention of building a cathedral. That never came to pass, and one of the city's finest oases became a public park on its transferral to Dublin City Council in 1974.

That last detail is one that makes the Joker's Chair (2002) so satisfying. Merrion Square isn't just a historical park. It's also something of an outdoor museum, with busts, memorials and even cobbles from old city streets used to edge its pathways (until recently, it also featured a selection of old city gas lamps). But the Joker's Chair is different – it's a bronze throne erected in honour of Dermot Morgan (1952–1998), the writer, satirist, actor and comedian best-known for playing *Father Ted* in the Channel 4 sitcom, and before that RTE's *Father Trendy*, and satirising various politicians on *Scrap Saturday*. Where there could have been a cathedral, in other words, there is now a throne honouring one of the funniest and most incisive critics of the Church that Ireland has seen.

Why a throne? Sculptor Catherine Green is obviously having fun, invoking absence and inviting passers-by to engage (have a seat!) while also being allegorical – evoking the Shakespearian fools that dished out cutting truths while the monarchs around them went ahead with their mad ideas anyway (we're looking at you, *King Lear*). 'Greene saw Dermot as being like the modern-day seer who never feared to tell the truth, cleverly, searingly and with verve', as it is put in the Dublin City Council guide *Art in Parks* (2014).

The inscription on the piece reads:

... and all the rest is laughter
laughter liberating
laughter to be remembered

IRISH ARCHITECTURAL ARCHIVE

The largest body of historical architectural records in Ireland

45 Merrion Square, Dublin 2
iarc.ie
Tuesday–Friday 10am–5pm
Admission: free
Pearse Street DART station (10-min walk); Luas, St Stephen's Green (Green Line; 10 to 15-min walk); Dublin Bus stops 409 and 493 are nearby on Merrion Square North

The Irish Architectural Archive collects and preserves the records of Irish architecture – from its earliest structures to contemporary buildings – and, as an independent limited company with charitable status, those records are freely available for anyone to consult.

The place to do that is a fitting one: the largest terraced townhouse on Merrion Square. This Georgian building dates from 1795, and after stepping through the automatic glass-door gateway, visitors arrive in a drawing room doused in natural light from several sash windows. This is the first exhibition space, where displays have ranged from architectural drawings of Leinster House to models of buildings designed by Eileen Gray (1878–1976), the Wexford-born architect most famous for E-1027, the holiday home she created with Jean Badovici on the French Riviera. Pushing through to a darker room inside, glass cabinets and subtle lighting might throw illumination on the work of architects like Pugin, for example, or on subjects ranging from Dublin's social housing to its Georgian interiors or the restoration of Christ Church Cathedral. Items in the collections range from books, pamphlets and drawings to the thousands of files created by larger practices.

Taken together, the archive's trove is the largest body of historical architectural records in Ireland, with over 250,000 drawings, 400,000-plus photographs and an extensive reference library in its care. Visitors can also access a huge range of books and periodicals, as well as early printed texts, using the catalogues and public-access terminals in the reading room.

NATIONAL PRINT MUSEUM

'Imagine what the world would be like without it …

Garrison Chapel, Beggars Bush Barracks, Haddington Road, Dublin 4
01 660-3770
nationalprintmuseum.ie
Tuesday–Friday: 10am–4pm; Saturday–Sunday: 12pm–4pm; closed
Mondays and bank holiday weekends
Lansdowne Road DART station (10–15-min. walk)

Print may be a medium in decline; this unusual jewel is anything but. Hidden away in a former chapel at Beggars Bush Barracks, the National Print Museum 'collects, documents, preserves, exhibits, interprets and makes accessible the material evidence of the printing craft, and fosters associated skills of the craft, in Ireland.' A wordy remit – and aptly so.

This is a working museum. Visit during term, and you might find schoolkids making posters, punching holes or folding origami printers' hats. You may be lucky enough to catch a retired printer demonstrating the machines he maintains. Guides are on hand to give tours ('Print was an even more important invention than the internet,' one says in passing) and you may even spot a student from the National College of Art and Design (NCAD) harnessing ideas for a letterpress project.

The history of printing dates all the way back to AD 105, when China's T'sai Lun developed paper from the shredded bark of a mulberry tree. In 1493 Johannes Gutenberg invented the printing press as we know it, and new technologies again came to the fore in the 1980s, when computers propelled print into the 21st century. Visitors to the museum can learn about the printing process, typefaces and the apprenticeships through which the craft was passed on, and even peruse one of the few surviving copies of the 1916 Proclamation of the Irish Republic. Typeset and printed in secrecy on an old Wharfedale stop-cylinder press (like the one on display in the museum), this is an intriguing document not just from a historical point of view, but also

as a record of the resourcefulness of the men who printed it. With a shortage in type supply, they mixed fonts, printed the document in two halves, used sealing wax to turn a 'P' into the 'R' of 'Republic' (check out the slightly fatter slanted leg) and worked late into the night that Easter Sunday. Only about 30 of the 1,000 original copies survive.

The museum has a clear message. Print may be dying in a digital age, physical newspapers and books may be fighting for their very survival, but the craft continues. 'Spend a week noting every printed item and object that you encounter or use,' it says. 'Then imagine what the world would be like without them. What a dull world it would be.'

WINDMILL LANE STUDIO TOUR

The ghosts of great rock n' roll

20 Ringsend Road, Dublin 4
windmilllanerecording.com
Hour-long tours must be booked in advance
Dublin Bus stops 355 (outbound) and 395 (towards the city centre) are very
close by (routes include 1, 15a, 15b, 47, 56a and 77a); the DART station at
Grand Canal Dock is a 5-min walk

There's a boxy old building beside the bus depot on Dublin's Ringsend Road. It looks forbidding, a bit like a bunker. But inside, some astonishing music has been recorded and mixed as the world walked by.

Think of Kate Bush's *Hounds of Love*, The Chieftains' *The Long Black Veil*, *The Commitments* soundtrack, or PJ Harvey's *To Bring You My Love*. All were recorded here. Lady Gaga, Ed Sheeran and AC/DC have also made history in the building. U2 cut *Zooropa* and *Pop* and mixed *Achtung Baby* in its studios too, as buses ground back and forth outside.

Today, the studio tour of the Windmill Lane Recording Studios is an intriguing and fun exploration of a building with a rock n' roll story for every step (Charlie Watts recorded drums for The Rolling Stones' *Voodoo Lounge* in the stairwell). Along the tour, you'll watch evocative videos, get a chance to work a mixing desk, place your ears at the 'sweet spot' like the engineers do, and sit for a photo op at the 72-channel Neve console in Studio One. That legendary space can fit an 80-piece orchestra … its wooden floor is also where Riverdance's steps were recorded. 'We have to have [music]', as former studio owner Brian Masterson put it. 'We can't live without it.'

Music fans may remember the old Windmill Lane. The original studio opened off the Liffey quays in 1978 – it was where an up-and-coming U2 recorded *Boy*, and fans later flocked to add graffiti to the walls (that building was demolished in 2015). The move to Ringsend came in 1990, to an unusual Art Deco building that had also housed a Bovril factory, a tramline depot power station and a snooker hall (in the middle of that Neve desk, an eight-ball from the old tables serves as a mouse. 'If it fits, it's meant to be', Masterson said). Don't miss the mementos on the walls, either. A framed fax from the Fugees, for example, reads: 'We have booked from 11pm through to early AM tomorrow, however expect anything to happen!'

A ghost story

Like all the best tours, this one comes with a ghost story, the tale of Cosmo, who died in the building. It's delivered with a difference, however – through lifelike, binaural recordings played through headphones.

CELTIC REVIVAL SYMBOLS

Romantic nationalism in Ringsend

The Oarsman, Ringsend, Dublin 4
theoarsman.ie
Sunday–Thursday 12noon–11.30pm, Friday and Saturday 12noon to
12.30am
Dublin Bus stops 356 and 392 are nearby on Bridge Street and are served by
routes 1 and 47; Grand Canal Dock DART station (15-min walk)

Ringsend is one of Dublin's forgotten inner-city suburbs, an outlier that never seems to have enough heritage, shops or restaurants to draw much interest from the city centre.

At its heart, however, lies Dublin's last surviving example of stuccowork portraying the ideals of romantic nationalism on a public house. You'll find it in the pediment of The Oarsman, a Victorian pub lying just across the road from St Patrick's Church. The decorative work takes the form of a roundel containing three quintessential symbols of Irishness – a round is, a Celtic cross and an Irish wolfhound – in true Celtic Revival style. What looks at first like whimsy is in fact the work of James Comerford and William Burnett, the renowned 19th-century stucco artists also responsible for the famed (though sadly defunct) Irish House on the Liffey quays. The simplistic, almost cartoonish depiction of the romantic nationalist symbols is a style that would have been popular in the city when it was created in the 1880s. It was commissioned when the pub was owned by William Tunney, and remained in place as the name changed from McCluskey's to McCarthy's and eventually its current incarnation as The Oarsman.

Inside, the pub is a nicely preserved Victorian oasis. Original features like whiskey casks with brass taps, a cast-iron support column, vintage grandfather clock and worn wooden floors all add authenticity and character, with the pick of the seating just inside a picture window overlooking the church. During the day, you can buy sandwiches and cakes as well as teas and coffees from a counter, or grab them to go from a window hatch facing onto Bridge Street.

GREAT SOUTH WALL

A direct line into Dublin Bay

Pigeon House Road, Ringsend, Dublin 4
Dublin Bus 18 (Sandymount/Palmerstown) stops at Seán O'Moore Road

Don't let first impressions fool you. Access to the Great South Wall is via one of the ugliest, smelliest and most industrial roads in the city. But that's just one of the factors that make it so special. Remember the scene towards the end of *The Shawshank Redemption* (1994), when Tim Robbins tunnels out of the prison, crawling through some 450m of subterranean shit pipes to taste freedom? It's kind of like that, only without the prison sentence.

Turning off the southside roundabout near the East Link toll bridge, take the first turn left into the industrial site. You'll pass scrapyards, power plants, container yards and a stinking sewage pond before the Pigeon House Road finally spits you out onto the capital's least-known stretch of coastline. Here, drive on round the Poolbeg Power Station until you come almost to the foot of the enormous Pigeon House Towers – the red-and-white-striped sentinels looking out over Dublin Bay. The Great South Wall stretches a couple of kilometres out into the bay, like a zip-line or a giant uvula ending at the Poolbeg Lighthouse. Park up, and you can enjoy a walk that transports you out into stunning views of the cityscape, the Howth peninsula, the Sugar Loaf in Wicklow, even Terminal 2 at Dublin Airport. Looking back towards Dublin from the end of the wall is an exhilarating sensation, especially on a windy day. Ferries and container ships pass on their way into Dublin Port. Kitesurfers billow about, like exotic birds. You're right in the middle of the bay.

The Great South Wall dates from 1716, when an original wood and gravel bulwark was commissioned to shelter incoming ships and combat the silting that plagued Dublin Bay. A stone version followed, using massive granite slabs from quarries at Dalkey. At the time of its completion in 1795, the 5km structure was one of the longest sea walls in the world – though much of it has since been gobbled up by Dublin's docklands. Despite its length, sand continued to thwart the shipping channel, so a sister wall (the Bull Wall) was constructed on the north side of the bay in 1824. Built after a survey by Captain William Bligh (of *Mutiny on the Bounty* fame), it combined with the Great South Wall to harness retreating tides, successfully scouring sand back out from the channel.

It's not only a hike, but a fascinating history lesson.

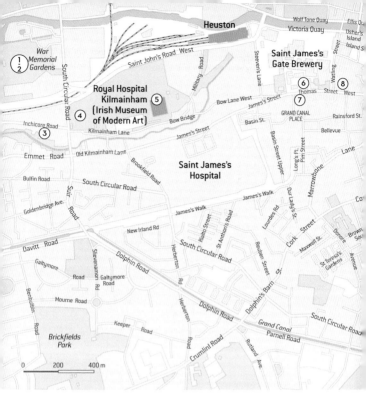

Wood Quay to War memorial

GUILLEMONT GINCHY CROSS ①

Sombre souvenirs from the Somme

War Memorial Gardens, Islandbridge,
Dublin 8
01 475-7816
heritageireland.ie
Monday–Friday 8am–sunset, Saturday & Sunday 10am–sunset
Access to bookrooms by appointment
Admission: free
Dublin Bus 51, 68, 69 from Aston Quay

O n 9 September 1916 some of the bloodiest fighting of the Somme campaign was brought to a close when the 16th Irish Division captured the villages of Guillemont and Ginchy. By then, the surrounding landscape had been transformed into a wasteland, so much so that an elm cross erected some months later, built from a beam of a shattered farmhouse in Flanders, would have been one of the few intact items – natural or manmade – for kilometres around.

Today, that cross stands hidden away within one of two granite bookrooms in the War Memorial Gardens. Call ahead for one of the attendants to open the metal doors, and a shaft of light spills inside, illuminating a tall, dark Celtic cross stretching some 4m in height inside. The Guillemont Ginchy Cross, as it is known, was made in December 1916 by the pioneer battalion of the 16th Irish Division, whose title and emblem – a shamrock – are engraved onto the crossbeam. A metal plate down the front surface appears to hold the wood together, and is spotted with smaller souvenir crosses pinned with paper poppies – mementos from visiting veterans and their families. Behind it hang several poppy wreaths.

According to a bronze plaque in the room, the memorial was placed on the Somme battlefield, between the villages of Ginchy and Guillemont, in February 1917. A sepia-tinted photograph shows the cross on its original site, with a small footnote reminding visitors of the terrible toll taken by this battle: during the capture of the two towns, the Irish Division's casualties amounted to 236 officers and 4,091 other ranks. The cross remained on the battlefield for nine years before being replaced by an Irish granite cross erected in church grounds at Guillemont in 1926. It was brought to Ireland 'with due reverence' in 1937.

Harry Clarke's hidden gem

War Memorial Gardens, Islandbridge,
Dublin 8
01 475-7816
heritageireland.ie
Monday–Friday 8am–sunset, Saturday & Sunday 10am–sunset
Access to bookrooms by appointment
Admission: free
Dublin Bus 51, 68 and 69 from Aston Quay

Ireland's War Memorial Gardens are well known, both as a stately commemoration of the soldiers who died in the First World War and as one of four Irish gardens designed by Sir Edwin Lutyens. Sunken rose gardens, sculpted lawns and pristine ornamental features combine to make a gorgeous space in which to play, pray or wallow.

Less well known are the two granite bookrooms at the gardens' heart. To access these, you need to call the park attendant in advance – or chance your luck on arrival – and once a time has been arranged, the attendant will meet you with a key. It's a rigmarole, but a very worthwhile one. Inside the southern pavilion, you'll find glass-topped cabinets containing *Ireland's Memorial Records* – eight volumes in which the names of Irish soldiers who died in the Great War are inscribed. Ireland might have been neutral, but that didn't stop 49,435 men from 'falling' between 1914 and 1918. Almost every town and village lost someone.

Soldiers are listed alphabetically in short entries along with their rank, regiment, place of birth and the date and cause of their death ('killed in action', 'died of wounds' and so on). The books are illustrated by Harry Clarke – the Arts & Crafts artist whose stained glass shines so beautifully elsewhere. Here, though lacking his usual vibrant explosions of colour, you'll find Clarke's signature artistry applied to a title page depicting Hibernia with her torch, wolfhound and harp, and margins strewn with Celtic symbols, silhouettes of soldiers and battlefield scenes. Hard as it may be to feel an emotional connection with men who died a century ago, the care in these books certainly succeeds in honouring them.

The volumes date from 1923, when 100 copies were commissioned following an appeal to gather the names of the Irish dead after the Great War. Published by Maunsel & Roberts, the books employed the best of contemporary Irish craftsmanship and were housed in the War Memorial Gardens when they opened in 1940 – ironically, just as another generation of young men were dying in the Second World War. Queen Elizabeth and Prince Philip visited in 2011 and their signatures are also on display.

KILMAINHAM MADONNA

Art behind bars

Kilmainham Gaol, Inchicore Road, Dublin 8
01 453-5984
heritageireland.ie – kilmainhamgaolmuseum.ie
October–March: 9.30am–5.20pm; April, May, September: 9.30–5.45pm;
June–August: 9.30–6pm; access by guided tour only (booking advised)
Luas, Suir Road (Red Line); Dublin Bus 69 and 79 from Aston Quay, and 13
and 40 from O'Connell Street, stop on Inchicore Road

Kilmainham Gaol made its mark on thousands of prisoners between the 1780s and 1920s, including many key figures from Irish history. But some also made their mark on the gaol.

One of its most famous female political prisoners was Grace Gifford (1888–1955), a Dublin-born artist and cartoonist best known for her relationship with the nationalist, Joseph Plunkett. Gifford was born a Protestant, but decided to become a Catholic after meeting the deeply religious Plunkett (his middle name was Mary, after the Blessed Virgin). The couple's wedding date was set for Easter Sunday of 1916 – rather inauspiciously, as it turned out, given Plunkett's leadership role in the 1916 Rising. When he was condemned to death, his fiancée brought a wedding ring to the chapel at Kilmainham Gaol, where the couple were married on the eve of his execution, 3 May. Gifford later returned as a prisoner in her own right, spending three months in 'A' Wing as a member of the anti-Treaty IRA. It was during this time that she painted the Kilmainham Madonna, a glowing mural of the Virgin and Child in pencil and watercolour that, deliberately or not, evokes her husband's name.

After being closed in 1923, Kilmainham Gaol lay abandoned for decades. During this time, the elements took their toll on Gifford's work, along with other historic graffiti, so the mural on view today is a 1966 restoration, painted by Thomas Ryan, later a President of the Royal Hibernian Academy of Arts. How accurately Ryan's retouching reflects the original is unclear, as Anne Clare writes in *Unlikely Rebels: The Gifford Girls and the Fight for Irish Freedom* (Mercier, 2011). 'He decided to change the Virgin's cloak from blue to red, and though she herself lacks the free-flowing gracefulness that characterised the original, the artist still avoided the relative lifelessness of the 20th-century Italian Madonnas.' You can decide for yourself by peering through the spy hole in Gifford's cell door during a guided tour.

BULLY'S ACRE

Dublin's oldest graveyard

Military Road, Kilmainham, Dublin 8
Military Historian and author Paul O'Brien runs occasional summer
tours of Bully's Acre, or groups can book tours by appointment
by emailing rhktours@opw.ie
Luas, Heuston (Red Line; 5-min. walk); Dublin Bus stop 2640 is nearby on
the Inchicore Road

Bully's Acre may be a quiet and peaceful corner of the city now, but in its heyday, Dublin's oldest graveyard was a very busy place – both by day and by night.

Set just inside the Royal Hospital's Kilmainham gate, the 2.4 hectare site has a long history. Bully's Acre was the location of a 12th-century priory founded by the Knights of St John of Jerusalem, and before that, Brian Boru and his troops are believed to have camped here before the Battle of Clontarf in 1014. Earlier still, it was the site of a monastery founded by St Maigneann (after whom Kilmainham, or *Cill Maigneann*, is named). 'Bully' is probably a corruption of the word 'bailiff'. As it was common ground, hundreds of thousands of people were laid to rest here over the centuries – 'monks, knights, princes and citizens', as an explanatory plaque puts it. Among them were the Irish nationalist leader Robert Emmet (for all of a few days), boxer Dan Donnelly and possibly even the sons of Brian Boru, who were killed at Clontarf. About 70 gravestones remain.

Bully's Acre was a favourite haunt of bodysnatchers. Indeed, Dan Donnelly's was one of countless corpses exhumed by the grave robbers supplying city surgeons with material for dissection in the 18th and early 19th centuries. 'An abundant supply is obtained for all Dublin schools from the burying ground commonly know as Bully's Acre,' as a medical student writing to *The Lancet* – quoted by Frank Hopkins in *Rare Old Dublin* (Marino, 2002) – claimed in 1830. 'There is no watch on this ground and subjects are to be got with great facility.' Public outrage led to the return of Donnelly's body (albeit minus an arm), but he was an exception – at the height of the trade, disinterred corpses were even being exported to the UK.

In 1832 Bully's Acre was finally closed to the public because of a cholera epidemic. If the gates are closed, the best spot for a view of the remaining headstones – which include a granite cross shaft dating from the 10th century – is halfway along the eastern wall, where it dips to a height of some 1.2m, giving a clear view over the leafy paddock inside.

ORDER OF THE GARTER MOTTO

'Evil be to him who evil thinks'

Royal Hospital, Military Road, Kilmainham, Dublin 8
01 612-9903
rhk.ie – imma.ie
Tuesday–Saturday 10am–5.30pm, Wednesday 10.30am–5.30pm,
Sunday noon–5.30pm
Admission: free
Luas, Heuston (Red Line; 10-min. walk); Dublin Bus stops 2637 and 2638
are nearby on St John's Road West, just after Heuston station

There's a story told about Edward III (1312–77) and a young woman he is said to have admired, the Countess of Salisbury. While attending a ball in Calais, the countess accidentally dropped her garter, provoking the amusement of the assembled company. Edward III, defending the lady's honour, is said to have picked up the garter, tied it around his own leg and pledged to found an order of knighthood in its name.

'*Honi soit qui mal y pense*,' he exclaimed. 'Evil be to him who evil thinks.'

Garters and evil may be far from the mind of visitors to the Royal Hospital. Built as a home for retired soldiers in 1684, this is one of the finest buildings of its period in Ireland – as well as the home of IMMA, the Irish Museum of Modern Art. Look closely at the steeple over the Great Hall, however, and you'll see a coat of arms under the pediment facing the formal gardens. It belongs to the Duke of Ormond, who commissioned the building, and is encircled by the same words: *Honi soit qui mal y pense*.

Although the story linking Edward III and the countess is probably untrue, the Order of the Garter – with its motto, also translated as 'Shamed be he who thinks evil of it' – is very real indeed. The oldest and most senior British order of chivalry, it honours those who have held public office, contributed to national life or served the sovereign personally (it's exclusive too, with numbers limited to 24, plus Royal Knights, at any one time). The order was founded by Edward III in 1348, although the garter itself is more likely to represent a belt or arming buckle, with the knot symbolising ties of loyalty, than a racy piece of underwear. James Butler, the Duke of Ormond, was a Knight of the Garter, hence his use of the motto at Kilmainham.

In an interesting footnote, Butler's grandson – also called James – was appointed a Knight of the Order of the Garter a few months after succeeding to the dukedom in 1688. After he was accused of supporting the Jacobite rising of 1715, however, his honours were extinguished. Butler's banner as a Knight of the Garter was taken down in St George's Chapel, in what remains the last formal degradation from the order, on 12 July 1716.

GUINNESS ARCHIVES

Arthur's archives

St James's Gate, Dublin 8
01 408-4800
guinness-storehouse.com
By appointment
Luas, St James's Hospital [Red Line; 10-min. walk]; Dublin Bus 123 runs
from O'Connell Street and Dame Street every 8–10 mins

The Guinness Storehouse is Ireland's most popular paid-for attraction. Year after year, the home of the Black Stuff bulges with over 1.7 million visitors, delivering a state-of-the-art brewery tour that culminates in a lesson on how to pull the perfect pint (it takes 119.53 seconds, apparently). But for all its flashy displays, the Storehouse story remains an overview. The rich details lie elsewhere … within its awesome archives.

Guinness dates back to 1759, when Arthur Guinness signed his famous 9,000-year lease. A trove of records has been maintained since that time, but it was only in 1998 that the Guinness Archives were formally established. Treasures are now kept in climate-controlled facilities ('If you were to lay out our papers end to end, they would stretch for about seven kilometres,' says Archive Manager, Eibhlin Colgan). Materials are accessible to Guinness marketing communities, economic and brewing historians, collectors, family history researchers 'and anyone with an interest in the Guinness Company and brand', but that doesn't mean you can simply swing by for a white gloves experience. Visitors need a solid reason and a specific request, with appointments given in a small room full of vintage bottles (both glass and stoneware) backstage in the Storehouse.

Even a small glimpse will give you goosebumps. There are tantalising black and white photographs of coopers at work, of barges being loaded on a Liffey dock, of draymen 'at tap' (chugging their daily beer allowance), of formally dressed Victorian master brewers. A small collection of artefacts on display includes the keg from which President Obama was served a pint of Guinness on his 2011 visit to Moneygall, Co. Offaly. On Secret Dublin's visit, treasures included an 18th-century Brewers' Guild minute book featuring Arthur Guinness's original signature, an Instagram-worthy trove of old pub labels, and original John Gilroy charcoal and watercolour sketches for iconic Guinness ads. Deep within the archives, there are barley grains from Tutankhamun's tomb and, of course, Arthur's original vellum lease (the indenture displayed in the Guinness Storehouse is a copy). Much like that perfect pint, it takes time for the scale of Ireland's largest private business archive to sink in.

Guinness is inextricably linked with the social and economic history of Dublin, and the archives also include paper records of 20,000 or so employees from the 1880s to the 1980s. 'When we started the service, I imagined genealogical queries would be mostly from our American and overseas visitors,' Colgan says. 'But it has actually been mainly Irish people themselves.'

CAMINO STARTING POINT

'May the road rise to meet you'

St James's Church, James's Street, Dublin 8
01 453-1143
stjamesparish.ie
Sacristy: Monday–Wednesday 9.30am–12.30pm
Dublin Bus stops 1941 and 1996 are nearby on James Street. Both stops are
served by routes 123, 13 and 40, travelling east or west

To modern pilgrims, the Camino de Santiago de Compostela (or Way of St James) is a trail that begins in southern France or northern Spain and ends at St James's reputed burial site at the Cathedral of Santiago de Compostela in Galicia.

Medieval pilgrims setting off on the Camino wouldn't have been privy to the delights of budget airlines, however. They viewed their journeys as beginning once they left home. In Ireland, the traditional starting (or departure) point on the Camino was St James's Gate, where a shrine to the saint was located at the western entrance to the city. Pilgrims had their passports stamped here before setting sail for northern Spain and, though few people now realise it, that tradition has never stopped. Camino passports can still be bought and stamped in Dublin today.

The main place to do this is St James's Church, outside of which hangs a small blue tile featuring a scallop – traditionally the emblem of St James, and carried by pilgrims both for symbolic and practical reasons, such as scooping water from springs. In the sacristy here, you can purchase a passport featuring an Irish blessing ('May the road rise to meet you'). The church's stamp is included too – one of many that pilgrims will collect at towns or *refugios* along their way, and which serve as proof of their journey once they reach Santiago. Passports can also be ordered online from the Camino Society Ireland (www.caminosociety. ie), as can a specially designed Guinness stamp from the Storehouse nearby.

Other Camino links in the city can be seen in the remains of the old chapter house at Christ Church, which would have been used to receive pilgrims; Bulloch Castle in Dalkey, where monks provided accommodation for travellers next to what was then Ireland's main port; and street names like Lazer Lane, which recall old quarantine stations for lepers.

St James's Church itself dates from 1844, when Daniel O'Connell – whose carved head can be seen wearing an Irish crown outside the main entrance – laid its foundation stone.

ST PATRICK'S TOWER
AND PEAR TREE

The ghost of whiskey distilleries past …

Digital Hub, Thomas Street, Dublin 8
thedigitalhub.com – roeandcowhiskey.com
Working hours (reception is just inside the Thomas Street gate)
Dublin Bus stops 1940 and 1997 are nearby at the junction of Thomas and
Watling Streets; Luas, Museum (Red Line; 10-min walk)

Guinness isn't the only drinks superpower associated with Dublin. Two years before Arthur Guinness signed his historic lease at St James's Gate, fellow businessman Peter Roe had bought a substantial site for a whiskey distillery nearby on Thomas Street. It did a bomb too, producing over 7 million litres of whiskey a year at its peak. Whiskey from the Roe Distillery was exported as far afield as Australia, and brought the family enough wealth to allow them to bankroll the refurbishment of Christ Church Cathedral in the 1880s. By that time, it was Ireland's largest exporter of whiskey and the beating heart of Dublin's 'Golden Triangle', alongside other brands like Powers and Jameson. The 20th century was less successful. Irish whiskeys struggled to modernise, to compete with Scottish whisky, and to deal with war at home and Prohibition abroad. Roe ceased production in 1926 Guinness took over the site in 1949, with the distillery buildings demolished in stages – making way for housing, car parks, office buildings and so on. Today, small distilleries have been returning to the Liberties thanks to the resurgence in Irish craft spirits, and visitors can take tours and tastings at a new Roe & Co Distillery (named after the former giant, but located in the old Guinness Power Station), Teeling Distillery at Newmarket, and the Pearse Lyons Distillery in the former St James's Church. One striking structure remains from Roe's heyday, however. Just inside the Thomas Street entrance to the Digital Hub, a 46-metre windmill stands almost unchanged (save for its blades) since 1757. At the time of its construction, this was the largest smock windmill in Europe, and its distinctive copper-clad cupola would have been visible for miles around. Look closely at the onion-shaped dome, and you'll see a flat, 1.2-metre-high depiction of St Patrick bearing a crozier and mitre. It's the reason the structure is also known as St Patrick's Tower.

Another feature of note is the pear tree at the windmill's base. Bolted to a wall for support, the tree is said to have been planted early in the 19th century, when it would have stood alongside the tower at the heart of the distillery. It's on the Tree Council of Ireland's list of heritage trees because of its unusual location and habitat value. There's no access to the windmill itself, but autumn visits to the pear tree may prove more fruitful …

ROBERT EMMET'S WHEREABOUTS

'Let no man write my epitaph ...'

St Catherine's Church, Thomas Street, Dublin 8
Tara Street DART station (20-min. walk); Luas, Four Courts (Red Line; 15-min. walk); Dublin Bus stops 1939 and 1998 are nearby on Thomas Street

As political oratory goes, Robert Emmet's speech from the dock takes some beating: 'When my country takes her place among the nations of the earth, then – and not until then – let my epitaph be written.' Over 200 years since it was delivered, the speech continues to retain its force and its 25-year-old author has become central to Irish nationalist lore.

Emmet was executed on 20 September 1803 at a gallows erected outside St Catherine's Church on Thomas Street. Dressed in black, the United Irishman is said to have handed his watch to the executioner and hung for 30 minutes before his light frame finally succumbed.

Afterwards, according to an account in *History Ireland* magazine, he was decapitated on a butcher's block, with the hangman holding up the bloody head for the assembled crowds to witness. A monument outside St Catherine's honours the patriot, but it's the less-heralded plaque at ground-level in front of the railings that people tend to miss – a heavily chipped stone highlighting the site of Emmet's death 'at the roadway opposite this tablet'.

Emmet's failed rebellion was only the beginning of his legend, of course. After a brief burial at Bully's Acre, his body was disinterred and whisked away to an unknown location. Various theories exist as to where this was – some favour the former Emmet family vault at St Peter's Church (now demolished) on Aungier Street; others the vaults of St Michan's; still others the grounds of the Priory in Rathfarnham, then home to his sweetheart Sarah Curran, but now a housing estate. Ireland may have taken her place among the nations, but without a body, it may be quite some time before that epitaph can finally be written.

Although the whereabouts of Robert Emmet's body remain a mystery, several of the United Irishman's personal effects survive. In the National Museum at Collins Barracks, you'll find his emerald ring and leather notebook, for example Emmet's writing desk is also owned by The Brazen Head, where he took rooms. Ironically, both he and his hangman drank at the pub, and after his death, according to Aubrey Malone's *Historic Pubs of Dublin* (New Island Books, 2001), morbid patrons took to watching the latter drink before requesting their drinks 'from the hangman's glass'.

Most gruesome of all, displayed at the Pearse Museum in Rathfarnham is the thick-set and heavily marked block on which Emmet is said to have been executed.

OUR LADY OF LOURDES GROTTO

Dublin's 'Grotto Lotto'

St Catherine's Church, Meath Street,
Dublin 8
01 454-3356
meathstreetparish.ie
Admission: free
Tara Street DART station (25-min. walk); Dublin Bus stops 5025 and 7412
(5-min. walk); Luas, Harcourt Street (Red Line; 15–20-min. walk)

Set outside the medieval walls of the city, Dublin's Liberties were traditionally answerable to several masters and placed under the protection of several saints. Even today, the area retains the feel of a world unto itself – a place where salt-of-the-earth traders rub shoulders with art and design students or rock 'n' roll residents like Imelda May, amidst a jumble of centuries-old churches, squiffy pubs and hip new cafes.

At the heart of the Liberties is St Catherine's, one of the oldest parishes in the city and a place where the Catholic faith continues to run deep. Dip down the alleyway beside the church on Meath Street, for instance, and you'll find a grotto dedicated to Our Lady of Lourdes. A church or shrine dedicated to St Catherine of Alexandria is said to have existed in this area of Dublin since Hiberno-Norse times, and today, stones have been stacked up into a cave-like formation. One section contains a recessed statue of Our Lady, another a little alcove where devotees light candles and reflect on a framed prayer.

'O ever immaculate virgin mother of Mary,' it begins. 'You know my wants, my troubles, my sufferings. Deign to cast on me a look of pity ...'

Mary herself is dressed in flowing blue and white, glancing skywards with a halo of glowing lights about her head and a golden string of rosary beads draped over her arm. Bouquets of flowers lie scattered about her feet, left by locals who trickle in and out through the day. Some stop a few feet back, whispering a Hail Mary under their breath. Others venture closer, perhaps popping a coin in the candle box. The 21st century seems a world away.

Beside the grotto, look out for the little souvenir and card shop, where you can buy mass cards, trinkets and tickets for the weekly 'Grotto Lotto'. Prizes worth several hundred euros go to weekly winners, with profits funnelled into church fundraising.

The foundation stone for St Catherine's Church was laid in 1852, but look up and you'll notice the spire is in a rather different, Art Deco style. It was added in 1958.

METRO BURGER SIGN

The sign that escaped the skip

Lucky's, 78 Meath Street, Dublin 8
luckys.ie
Monday–Friday 4pm to close; Saturday from noon; Sunday from 2pm

'It's charmingly shite', John Mahon muses. Mahon is one of the owners of Lucky's, a modern neighbourhood-style bar in the Liberties, and he's talking about the Metro Burger sign in the beer garden. This large, octagonal piece might seem like a funky background feature. As with so much in Dublin, however, there's a surprising story behind it. 'It wasn't interesting at the time', as he says. 'It just became interesting over time.'

Metro Burger was a 1980s eatery attached to The Screen cinema. It closed in the 1990s, but the sign hung on, watching over huddles of people waiting for buses on Hawkins Street for decades. The 2016 closure of The Screen itself brought a fresh threat, however. Previously the New Metropole (a name echoed in Metro Burger, intentionally or otherwise), this boxy but beloved three-screen theatre showed art-house and foreign language films rather than the mainstream fare of its sister, The Savoy on O'Connell Street. Suddenly, with plans for its demolition and redevelopment, the whole lot looked set for the skip.

It wasn't. Emma Clarke of the *Dublin Ghost Signs* blog contacted the developers, and was told the sign could be taken as long as it was available 'for people to enjoy', as she told *The Journal* in 2019. She was joined in the project by Mahon, who also runs the blog *TheLocals.ie*, and Simon Kingston of design outfit Reverb. 'There's so little left from that particular moment in time, this [was] definitely like nostalgia for the three of us involved', Mahon says. 'We were kids in the '80s.' Over time, he explains, the sign came to take on the glow of an artefact that spoke to a pre-Internet, less international city – a touch point from 'a time when we were finding our feet and becoming a bit more wise to the world'.

The frame fell apart as soon as it was handled, he recalls. But the Perspex panels held together. Kingston made a new housing; the 'cack-handed' typeface and timeworn look was left as it was (including marks from where the lettering was taped out and printed). A fluorescent light was added, and the sign was then popped onto its pedestal at Lucky's. 'It's crude, but it's charming because of it', Mahon says today. 'I always like the fact that it just sort of survived despite everything that was going on around it … It was a survivor, a time capsule of how things used to look back in 1980s Dublin.'

MOSAICS OF JOHN'S LANE CHURCH

A poem in stone …

Church of St Augustine & St John, 94 Thomas Street, Dublin 8
01 677-0393; johnslane.ie
Monday–Friday 10am–5pm, Saturday 10am–6pm, Sunday 8.30am–1pm
Admission: free
Tara Street DART station (20–25-min. walk); Dublin Bus stop 1938 is
nearby; Luas, Four Courts (Red Line; 5–10-min. walk)

John's Lane Church makes an instant impression. Rising up near the ancient junction of Cornmarket, its red sandstone, granite and limestone façade tapers into a French Gothic steeple that remains, at over 60m, the tallest in the city. Although not as well-known as the nearby cathedrals, Pugin's design is one of the finest pieces of ecclesiastical architecture in the city – indeed, Ruskin is said to have dubbed it 'a poem in stone'.

Oohs and aahs abound. Outside, look for the 12 apostles in the nooks of the tower carved by James Pearse, father of the patriots Padraig and Willie. Inside, a soaring suite of arches and pillars carries the eye towards a bloom of stained glass windows and an altar cut from Carrara

marble. The contrast with the hustle and bustle of the Liberties is titillating. In a couple of bounds, you pass from a vigorous throng of arts students, from busy locals and street vendors selling everything from hula hoops to kitchen roll, into a sanctified space full of votive lights, carved confessional booths and twinkling shrines. John's Lane Church is no museum space, either. Visit during working hours, and you'll find a congregation kneeling with their priest, a cleaner running her mop across the marble, or hear the hushed verses of a rosary.

Amid all of this, it's easy to overlook the Shrine of Our Lady of Good Counsel. Set to the right of the altar as you face it, the little enclave is home to some breath-taking mosaics – with countless flecks of coloured glass and tiles arranged into crisp depictions of the Nativity and the Annunciation. An intricate take on the Augustinian crest is embedded into the floor; a painting of Mary and the infant Jesus forms the centrepiece above.

Dating from 1898, the enclave was tended throughout the 20th century by the 'Knights of the Shrine', who worked as ushers and stewards during novenas and other special devotions to Our Lady. Only a handful of these Knights remains – you might spot one or two at the annual Triduum (three-day devotion) to Our lady in April.

More intricate mosaics can be found in the Shrine of St Rita of Cascia (under the Harry Clarke window) and the Shrine of the Sacred Heart.

A STREET SIGN WITHOUT A STREET

The place that vanished

Oliver Bond Street, Dublin 8
Dublin Bus Stops 1938 and 1999 are nearby on Thomas Street; several other buses stop on Merchant's and Usher's Quays

A strect sign on Oliver Bond Street, sitting above the doorway of today's Liberties Training Centre, reads 'Mullinahack'. But there is no street, or area, to speak of here with that name. So what's the story?

Muileann an Chaca is the Irish translation provided. Muileann means mill, while 'cac' is an Irish word for crap, excrement or a dirty or worthless thing. Those two clues come together nicely in the title of a detailed essay on the area by Edward Hannon in the *Dublin Historical Record* (2016) – '*The unclean mills: Mullinahack – the place that vanished*'.

Mullinahack's origins appear to lie in a mill or mills which were located in the area for several centuries from the late 1100s. In its heyday, this 'once-vibrant neighbourhood' sprawled towards today's Usher's Quay and over parts of NCAD, and was traversed by a river named Coleman's Brook. The river was a real stinker, by all accounts, due to run-off from the mills and rampant local dumping. Another article in the *Dublin Historical Record*, written by Lily M O'Brennan in 1940, describes it as 'a much-abused stream' that was eventually 'cut off' for this reason around 1670. But the name Mullinahack lingered, of course. Hannon notes that in 1798 in the House of Lords, the Earl of Carhampton at one point described it as 'too vulgar for pronunciation, and scarcely to be articulated without the risk of breaking gentlemen's teeth'.

Subsequently, Mullinahack was home to a sugar refinery, and a railway carriage and coach makers, along with smaller industries such as hat and pipe-making (one famous resident was Anne Devlin (1780–1851), the Irish Republican also famous for being housekeeper to Robert Emmet). By the late 19th century, however, it was a place rife with crime, sanitation issues, and dotted with dodgy shebeens and boarding houses. Mullinahack Lane was eventually closed by Dublin Corporation in 1900. 'But its memory yet lingers', as O'Brennan observed in her piece four decades later. 'For its murky waters gave the name Mullinahack – the Dirty Mill – to a street, and even today the residents of St Augustine Street still call it by the old name.'

Today, the name barely hangs on, and all these stories have shrunk to the size of a mere street sign. But you can still find evidence of Mullinahack on old maps of the city, and evocative images in the National Library's archive.

THE 40 STEPS

The gateway to hell

Cook Street, Dublin 8
Tara Street DART station (15–20-min. walk); Luas, Four Courts (Red Line; 10-min. walk); Dublin Bus stops 1937 and 2001 are nearby on High Street

The faithful in Dublin's old churches worked hard to get into heaven, but the road to hell was all downhill. Literally. A medieval shortcut skirting around St Audeon's Church meant 40 steps was all it took for 18th-century citizens to descend from the heights of Cornmarket to a squalid pocket of brothels, taverns and laneways colloquially known as 'Hell'.

Stretching from Cook Street towards Fishamble Street, 'Hell' ran thick with criminals, outcasts and ne'er-do-wells – one of the most famous was Darkey Kelly, a notorious madame who ran the Maiden Tower brothel. As the story goes, Kelly became pregnant with the child of Dublin Sheriff, Simon Luttrell, and pressed him for financial support. Gentleman as he was, Luttrell denied all knowledge of the child and upped the ante by accusing his lover of witchcraft and infanticide. In 1761 Kelly was burnt at the stake in front of a baying mob, although the baby's body was never produced. She hasn't gone away, either – sightings of Darkey Kelly's ghost have been reported at the 40 Steps in the ominous passageway where abandoned babies were once left at the side of St Audeon's Church.

Interestingly, contemporary newspaper reports appear to suggest that Kelly may have been executed for another reason. Several bodies were discovered hidden in the vaults of her brothel, according to a recent rereading of reports by the producers of *No Smoke Without Hellfire* on Dublin South 93.9FM. Kelly may not have been a witch, in other words, but she may well have been Ireland's first serial killer. Welcome to hell, indeed.

Even today, the 40 Steps retain a dank, spooky atmosphere. No matter how bright the day, the thickness of the old city walls casts a pall over the bottom steps, and a long portion of the slipway is hidden from view – a fact that has not only proven attractive to historical criminals and drug addicts, but their contemporaries too. Be careful.

PORTLESTER CHAPEL AND CENOTAPH

A secret city centre space

St Audeon's Church, High Street, Dublin 8
01 677-0088
heritageireland.ie
May–October, daily 9.30am–5.30pm
Admission: free
Tara Street DART station (15–20-min. walk); Luas, Four Courts (Red Line;
10-min. walk); Dublin Bus stops 1937 and 2001 are nearby on High Street

Dating from 1181, St Audeon's is named after the patron saint of Normandy, St Ouen. But it doesn't take much nosing around this wonderful mash-up of medieval churches and chapels to find another name standing out: that of Roland FitzEustace, Lord Porlester.

In its golden age, St Audeon's was a wealthy parish in the commercial heart of Dublin. Burial here was a plum posthumous status symbol, and names like Usher, Sparke and Duff can still be found carved into large and wordy tombstones. FitzEustace, however – who was appointed Lord Chancellor of Ireland by both Edward IV and later Henry VII – went a step further. In 1455 he built his own private chapel. Hidden away just to the right of the visitor centre entrance, you'll find the space hemmed in by an elegant miscellany of medieval walls, Romanesque arches and the towering bulk of the neighbouring Catholic church. The chapel has been shorn of its roof since 1773, and an information panel includes a fading reproduction of George Petrie's 'Hanging Washing in Lord Porlester's Chapel', a painting of a woman stringing garments along lines across the arcade. It's a blithe, almost pastoral scene, remarkable for the fact that it takes place bang in the middle of Dublin.

The chapel and chancel were vested in the Board of Public Works in 1880, the panel goes on to reveal, at a time when the windows and arches were repaired and the tombstones laid horizontally.

The centrepiece of Portlester's chapel was a striking cenotaph. It was moved inside for protection many years ago, and today you'll find it in the bell tower, where recumbent effigies depict the baron in medieval knight's garb, with a sword hung from his hip, wife at his side and a loyal dog at his feet. Portlester commissioned it during his lifetime, but he is actually buried in Kilcullen, Co. Kildare.

MEDIEVAL LANEWAY

The only excavated example in the city

St Audeon's Church, High Street, Dublin 8
01 677-0088
heritageireland.ie
May–October, daily 9.30am–5.30pm
Admission: free
Tara Street DART station (15–20-min. walk); Luas, Four Courts (Red Line; 10-min. walk); Dublin Bus stops 1937 and 2001 are nearby on High Street

Y ou can view St Audeon's Church from above on High Street or from below on Cook Street, but neither gives a clue as to the layers of history hidden within. Dublin's only remaining medieval parish church dates from the 12th century (and possibly even before) and is riddled with nooks and crannies, with aisles, chapels, towers, tombs and monuments.

Right in the middle of St Anne's Chapel, you'll even find an excavated section of a 12th-century laneway. Dublin would have been braided with cobbled lanes when the medieval church was built, of course, but this claims to be the city's only excavated example showing a surviving section in its unaltered state. Discovered during the early 1990s, the lane is thought to have run close to the wall of the original church, and beneath the extensions that were added in subsequent centuries. It continued downhill towards the River Liffey, passing through St Audeon's Arch in the old city walls. Although only a short section is on display, curving slightly as its dark stones dip back underground, it's easy to imagine the pitter-patter of ancient feet. High Street and St Audeon's lay at the crossroads of medieval Dublin and all manner of tradespeople, laymen, priests and even pilgrims getting their passports stamped before embarking on the Camino would have used the timeless thoroughfare.

St Audeon's is at once a working parish church, and an Office of Public Works (OPW) heritage site. That's the beauty of a visit: in the Church of Ireland aisle, you'll find a spotless altar and an 11th-century baptismal font. Parallel to it in the Guild Chapel of St Anne, there's an exhibition on the medieval guilds that thrived in the church's heyday, with displays including a handful of instruments from the guild of barber surgeons – among which is a cauterising tool.

'The yron is most excellent but that it is offensive to the eye and bringeth the patient to great sorrowe and dread of the burning and the smart,' reads a contemporary account.

HOLY WATER STOOPS

Symbolic seashells

St Audeon's Catholic Church, High Street, Dublin 8
087 239-3235
kosciol-dublin.pl
Tara Street DART station (15–20-min. walk); Luas, Four Courts (Red Line;
10-min. walk); Dublin Bus stops 1937 and 2001 are nearby on High Street

Dating from 1846, St Audeon's Catholic Church (as distinct from the Church of Ireland next door) is home to the Polish Chaplaincy in Ireland. Several minor gems are found inside, including a handcrafted Walker organ dating from 1861 and a statue of the Infant Jesus carved by Pietro Bonanni in 1847, but the most unusual are just outside the door. Holy water stoops set either side of St Audeon's front entrance are actually enormous clamshells, fished from the Pacific Ocean in 1917, as the story goes, and brought back to Dublin by a seaman whose brother was one of the parish priests working in the church at the time.

Shells are not an uncommon motif in churches, of course. Throughout antiquity, hinged species like the scallop and clam have symbolised fertility and the female – both as protective and nurturing forms, and more explicitly as emblems of the vulva. The scallop, for instance, was the symbol of Venus. Although it's not mentioned in the bible, Christian tradition also has it that John used a clamshell to baptize Jesus, and shells can often be found decorating baptismal fonts or used to pour Holy Water over babies. Giant clams are the world's largest molluscs, living in the wild for a century or more and weighing up to 200kg in their prime. In some cases, giant specimens like those at St Audeon's are even used as baptismal fonts.

Although made from stone, a 12th-century baptismal font featuring a seashell carved on its aisle-facing side is still in use at St Audeon's Church of Ireland next door.

Visitors may linger at its unique holy water stoops today, but taking one's time wasn't always the St Audeon's way. This church was where, from the 1950s, Father 'Flash' Kavanagh was reputed to say the fastest Sunday mass in the city, freeing parishioners in time for The Sunday Game!

WOOD QUAY AMPHITHEATRE

Echoes of history

Dublin City Council Civic Offices, Wood Quay, Dublin 8
dublincityartsoffice.ie
Daylight hours (park)
Admission: free
Tara Street DART station (15-min. walk); Dublin Bus stops 2001 (High Street) and 1444 (Wood Quay) are serviced by numerous routes from the city centre

Dublin's Civic Offices are its most controversial buildings. Built atop of one of the most significant Viking archaeological sites in Europe, architect Sam Stephenson's brutalist-style 'bunker' structures are as bull-headed a symbol of 'progress' as you'll find in the city.

They didn't go up without a fight. As construction loomed in the late 1970s, officialdom locked horns with an outraged Irish public in an unprecedented way. Up to 20,000 protestors, including the young (future President) Mary Robinson, took to the streets in 'Save Wood Quay' marches. As excavations continued, Professor F.X. Martin and his 'Friends of Medieval Dublin' even occupied the site. In the end, the campaign failed, excavated treasures went to the National Museum and two of four planned 'bunkers' were built (the river-facing block by Scott Tallon Walker was added in 1994). Arguably, however, Ireland's attitude towards preserving its heritage had changed for ever.

Moseying through the park and pathways linking the buildings today, the historical footnote springs to life. Was the right decision made? What was the alternative? Parts of the landscaping do evoke some optimism – especially the public amphitheatre that nestles up against the 'bunkers'. Rows of granite seating and a raised, circular stage surrounded by grass verges set a sweet scene for a picnic or coffee, and in summer, the amphitheatre hosts outdoor events. Opera in the Open, for example, is a Dublin City Council initiative presenting live performances every Thursday lunchtime during August. Other one-off events take place from time to time – on Culture Night in September, for instance. Lurking in the building behind is the indoor Wood Quay Venue, a basement meeting and exhibition space that incorporates a stretch of 12th-century city walls uncovered during the construction.

If you fancy venting your frustration, do it in the centre circle of the amphitheatre. Shout, or sing, in this exact spot, and your voice will echo in the most surprising way. Step out of the circle and the echo ends. It's a space that resonates in more ways than one.

THE CAT AND THE RAT

Tom and Jerry ...

Christ Church Crypt, Christchurch, Dublin 2
01 677 8099
christchurchcathedral.ie
Opening hours vary by month, but generally start from around 10am
weekdays and 12.30pm Sundays
Tara Street DART station (10 to 15-min walk); Luas, Smithfield (10-min
walk); Dublin Bus stops 2002 and 2035 are nearby on Lord Edward Street
and Nicholas Street

Christ Church Cathedral is one of the stand-out structures in Dublin, a granite chandelier of a centrepiece that could hold its own in any city on earth.

Although founded by the Hiberno-Norse King Sitric in 1028, today's architecture has been heavily influenced by extensive Victorian restorations. It's sometimes hard to tell whether you're looking at an elegant Anglo-Norman original, a Victorian pastiche – or what's really the case, a spectacular hodgepodge of both.

One part of the building that hasn't been interfered with is the crypt. The oldest surviving structure in Dublin stretches under both the nave and choir of the cathedral, and its nooks and crannies are home to some unique treasures: a plate gifted by William of Orange after the Battle of the Boyne (1690), medieval city stocks dating from 1670 (they were once used to punish criminals on Christ Church Place) and the reputed tomb of Strongbow among them. Most surprising of all, however, are the mummified cat and mouse displayed in a glass case. The parched, leathery creatures were found trapped in one of the church's organ pipes in the 1860s, where local lore suggests they became stuck during a high-speed chase and were subsequently preserved in the dry atmosphere of the crypt. Tom and Jerry, as they are known, were discovered during a servicing of the organ and went on to find themselves name-checked in James Joyce's *Finnegans Wake*, where a character is described as 'stuck as that cat to that mouse in that tube of that Christchurch organ'.

While you're browsing through the crypt's motley artefacts, take a moment to look around at the arches and columns supporting this 12th-century maze. Many centuries after their construction, they continue to take the weight of the entire cathedral.

On 13 April 1742, Handel's Messiah debuted at Neal's Musick Hall, across the road on Fishamble Street. The oratorio was rapturously received, and the original entrance arch and a plaque commemorating the event can be found by Handel's Hotel. Anniversary performances have taken place here.

SYNOD HALL BRIDGE

From Vikings to vaults

Winetavern Street, Dublin 8
Christ Church: 01 677-8099; christchurchcathedral.ie
Opening hours vary by month, but generally start from around 10am
weekdays and 12.30pm Sundays
Dublinia: 01 679-4611; dublinia.ie
Daily 10am–5.30pm

Tara Street DART station (10–15-min. walk); Luas, Smithfield (Red Line;
10-min. walk); Dublin Bus stops 2002 and 2035 are nearby on Lord Edward
Street and Nicholas Street

For a city that is rained upon so often, Dublin doesn't really 'do' covered walkways. When it does, however, it does them in style – as with this arching, integrated bridge linking Christ Church Cathedral and its former Synod Hall over Winetavern Street.

The bridge dates back to the 1870s, when it was added during extensive renovations undertaken by George Edmund Street. This was also when the Synod Hall was built around the former St Michael's Church – the two buildings were unrelated at the time and Street designed the Synod Hall to incorporate St Michael's original 12th-century tower. The hall itself was 'large and prosaic', as Christine Casey describes it in *Dublin* (Yale University Press, 2005), but the bridge is an unexpected delight. Caen stone walls and a timber roof are offset by a series of leaded stained glass windows that let in floods of pixelated light whenever there's a blast of sunshine. On one wall, a shining plaque remembers Henry Roe, the wealthy distiller at whose 'sole expense' the Synod Hall was erected. It's a surprising and atmospheric treat enhanced by the sense of remove from the busy stream of cars and buses passing below.

Today, the Synod Hall is occupied by Dublinia, an interactive exhibition about the medieval city. Combined tickets can be bought for Dublinia and Christ Church, allowing visitors to exit the exhibition on an upper floor, cross over the bridge and descend via the smooth limestone steps into the cathedral. Alternatively, one can access the structure via Christ Church itself, though confusingly, Dublinia cannot be entered from the east this way.

TAILORS' HALL

The Back Lane Parliament

An Taisce, Back Lane, Dublin 8
antaisce.org
Admission free (via the café if events are not taking place; otherwise groups can have tours during office hours, by appointment)
Tara Street DART station (15-min walk); Dublin Bus 2001 stops nearby on High Street

Just a single medieval guildhall survives in Dublin. Squirrelled away in the aptly named Back Lane, off High Street, the two-storey building has most recently been home to An Taisce, the National Trust for Ireland.

Without its intervention, it's unlikely that Tailors' Hall would be here at all. The building dates from 1706, when the Guild of Merchant Tailors established it as its headquarters and meeting place. Back then, Dublin was a radically different city. Today's High Street streams with six lanes of traffic, and busy junctions make it tough work for pedestrians. When the city's tailors visited their HQ, however, they would have come at it through a tight-knit neighbourhood dotted with markets, tanneries, taverns, breweries and linen shops, with long-vanished names like Cutpurse Row and Handkerchief Alley (a small chunk of the old City Walls remains on Lamb Alley). Tailors met here until 1841, and in their day were an influential guild. 'They had the right, for instance, to seize the cloths of tailors who were not members of the guild but were selling in the city', as Peter Pearson writes in *The Heart of Dublin* (O'Brien Press, 2000). But, of course, that was then.

This is now. Over the years, Cornmarket and the junctions near Christ Church were overhauled. Whole streets were razed; others widened and re-landscaped. Tailors' Hall went through various different uses – as an army barracks, hostel and courthouse, for instance – before being left to rot. An Taisce's restoration is a minor miracle, and it was a deserved winner of the Europa Nostra Award in 1988.

So what can you see today? Rich red brick and surprisingly grand arched windows hint at the history within. The Great Hall contains a minstrels' gallery with a sparse, wrought-iron balustrade and large marble fireplace (look for the 18th-century engravings; sadly, the central tablet has been stolen). At the time of this guide's latest update, a new café was set to open, bringing new life to the building. It's not just about built heritage, either. In 1792 Wolfe Tone, James Napper Tandy and others met here during a campaign against the Penal Laws, leading to its nickname: the Back Lane Parliament.

LORD IVEAGH'S LIKENESS

Lord Iveagh's 'impish' grin

Iveagh Market, 22–27 Francis Street,
Dublin 8
Dublin Bus stop 2383 is on nearby Patrick Street, with stop 7413 also nearby
at The Coombe; Luas, Harcourt Street (Green Line; 15-min. walk)

Sir Edward Cecil Guinness (1847–1927), also known as Lord Iveagh, certainly made his mark on Dublin. But could this kooky-looking keystone, set into one of the arches ringing the Iveagh Markets, be the most personal mark of all?

The figure is one of several carved into the keystones on the former market building. The keystones represent the continents, according to Christine Casey's *Dublin* (Yale University Press, 2005), but Pat Liddy, the legendary Dublin author and tour guide, has suggested that the 'impish grin' of the bearded figure appearing to wink at passers-by from the corner of Francis Street and Dean Swift Square is that of Lord Iveagh, who founded the Iveagh Trust to provide affordable housing in Dublin and London.

The Iveagh Trust was established in 1890 and its legacy in Dublin is astonishing. Overlooking St Patrick's Park (created by Sir Benjamin Guinness), you'll find a beautiful complex of buildings including the Iveagh Trust Flats, the famous 'Bayno' where local children played, and the Iveagh Baths, which housed a swimming pool for residents. The Iveagh Market dates from 1906, when it was commissioned to accommodate street traders who had lost their old market rights after inner-city slums were cleared. Designed by Frederick G. Hicks, the covered market was for traders selling old clothes, fish, fruit and vegetables, and was built on a site formerly occupied by Sweetman's Brewery. Beyond its brick and stone façade lies a market hall with a perimeter gallery perched on cast-iron columns.

The market continued in operation until the 1990s but has lain sadly derelict for some time. A redevelopment scheme was mooted, but it has recently been the subject of a legal dispute between the developer, Dublin City Council and Lord Iveagh.

Though the building's fortunes have waxed and waned, the winking keystone remains. Perhaps it knows something we don't?

CITY WALLS

If these walls could talk …

Power's Square, off St Nicholas Street, Dublin 8
Tara Street DART station (20-min. walk); Luas, St Stephen's Green (Green
Line; 10-min. walk); Dublin Bus 49 stops nearby on St Nicholas Street

At first glance, Power's Square seems noteworthy only for its pretty inner-city gardens. Take a closer look at the trees and blooms marking the eastern end of this tiny enclave, however, and you'll see a 4m wedge of stone hiding in plain sight. It's as solid a chunk of history as you'll find in the city – a surviving section of the old City Walls.

The 68m stretch of the old wall alignment, altered over time but still containing some of its original masonry, is one of few remaining sections of Dublin's medieval defences. Other sections, such as the early mural defences on Cook Street, the 83m stretch at Ship Street Lower and the monument-style remnant on Lamb Alley at Cornmarket, may be better known – but similarly to Power's Square, they survived because they were incorporated into later property boundaries. Without that, all would have long since vanished.

Most of the remaining City Walls, which John Perrot's survey of 1585 describes as having measured between 4.8m and 6.7m high and between 1.22m and 2m wide, are buried beneath the modern city. Remnants have been found during archaeological investigations at City Hall, Dublin Castle, Werburgh Street, Nicholas Street, Winetavern Street, Augustine Street and Usher's Quay among other locations. A section of the early mural defences survives in the basement of Dublin's Civic Offices at Wood Quay. Dublin Castle's Record Tower is another survivor, as is the base of Bermingham Tower and the foundations of the Powder Tower, which visitors can see in an underground chamber during castle tours. Elsewhere, the remains of Genevel's Tower are

preserved within an underground chamber at Ross Road, although not currently accessible to the public. On Exchange Street Lower, the base of Isolde's Tower can also be seen in a murky holding area beneath an apartment block.

If you're interested in learning more about the route of the City Walls, it's possible to follow the 'virtual' perimeter via a series of granite markers dotted at various points around the historic city centre. Bronze plaques on the markers contain an outline of the medieval city, with metal spots denoting the location of particular towers and gates.

CHURCH OF ST NICHOLAS OF MYRA (WITHOUT)

Santa Claus and the Axe Murderers

Francis Street, Dublin 8
01 454-0387
francisstreetparish.ie
Monday–Friday: 9.30am–noon; Saturday 9.30am–noon; 4.30pm–6.30pm;
Sunday: 10am–noon
Dublin Bus stop 2383 is on nearby Patrick Street, with stop 7413 also nearby
at The Coombe; Luas, Harcourt Street (Green Line; 15-min. walk)

To step into the Church of St Nicholas of Myra is to step back in time.

Arrive around 10.30am midweek, just after mass has wound up, and you may find a small congregation intoning the rosary. Old women massage their beads with waxy, wrinkled fingers, while around them, a suprisingly beautiful interior blooms like a flower.

Dating from 1829, the church has its origins in a 13th-century Franciscan monastery. The 'Without' part of its title refers to the fact that it lay outside the medieval city walls, as distinct from the Church of St Nicholas of Myra (Within). Hidden away in a sprawl of inner-city housing, its immaculately maintained interior is dotted with little alcoves and shrines, bright statues of Jesus, Mary, Joseph and St Anthony. Over the altar, a Pietà by sculptor John Hogan shows Christ laid out after his crucifixion, his mother about to cup his head in her hands. Rich stained-glass windows include Harry Clarke's depiction of the marriage of Mary and Joseph, and St Nicholas of Myra with three golden satchels and an anchor at his feet – hinting at his role as Santa Claus and the patron saint of sailors. Pews line up neatly beneath a beautifully ornate ceiling, raspberry-pink recessed panels pick up the curtains in the confessional booths, and a line of plaster friezes skirts behind the altar and its flickering candles. A thought for the day reads: 'One of the secrets of life is to make stepping stones out of stumbling blocks.'

On your way into the building, don't miss its map of medieval Dublin. It shows the locations of various churches dedicated to St Nicholas through the ages, along with a hilarious illustration from Giraldus Cambrensis's *Topography of Ireland* (1188). Entitled 'Irishmen Demonstrate the Axe', it depicts a crazy-eyed savage who, despite the presence of an eminently chop-able tree, 'demonstrates' his tool by lodging it in his colleague's forehead.

Like its namesake beyond the old city walls, the Church of St Nicholas (Within) has a long history dating back to the 11th century. Its fortunes ebbed and flowed over the centuries, and sadly, all that remains of it today is a bricked-up portion of its entrance at the junction of Nicholas Street and Christchurch Place, by the city's Peace Park.

BRONZE PLAQUES

'I'll cure you myself'

Nicholas Street, Bride Street, Bride Road, & Ross Road,
Dublin 8
chrisreidartist.com
Tara Street DART station (20-min. walk); Luas, Harcourt Street (Green Line;
10-min. walk); Dublin Bus stops 2385 and 2310 are nearby

'I never really had a conversation with my father. Sometime in the 1960s he caught me mitching from school and gave me an awful hiding. Ripped the clothes off me, lashed me with the belt and punched me in the eyes.'

It's the kind of revelation you'd wince at in a book, an interview, or perhaps were it to be delivered in confidence over a cup of tea or a pint. And yet here they are … the same words, cast in bronze in a plaque set into the walls of Nicholas Street. Nor are they alone. Keep your eyes peeled as you walk past the redbrick Victorian flats of Bride Street, Bride Road and Ross Road, and you'll find 20 or so others set into the streetscape. Sobering confessions, nuggets of social history and memories of the rare ol' times: these are walls that really do talk.

The plaques are based on recordings made by artist Chris Reid with local residents and installed as a commission under Dublin City Council's Public Art Programme. By casting them in bronze, and giving them a heritage-style appearance you might normally associate with official tributes or memorials, Reid further emphasises the fact that voices like these are so rarely heard. One local remarks on how good it would be if a community centre were to be built in the area. Others remember camaraderie in the pubs, local men taking bets as they tossed coins into a pot behind the Iveagh Baths, neighbours teaming up to wash their stairs, or the local ragman who tricked kids into swapping valuable clothes for goldfish.

Professor Declan McGonagle of the University of Ulster has suggested that the results 'ventilate history from within'. And certainly, these insights into a world out of sight for so many Dubliners can be startling in their simplicity. 'My mother didn't believe in doctors,' another reads. 'She couldn't afford to pay them anyway. All the mothers were the same. They had these old-fashioned remedies. 'I'll cure you myself,' my mother used to say.'

Since installing the plaques in 2009, Reid has published a book – *Heirlooms & Hand-me-downs* – that develops the stories and memories.

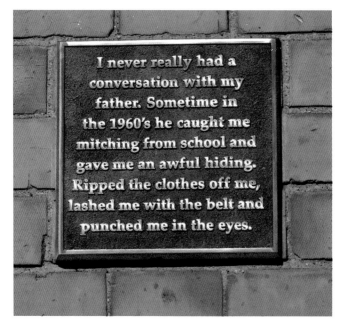

THE MUSEUM FLAT

The flat that's frozen in time

3B Iveagh Trust, Patrick Street, Dublin 8
01 454-2312 – theiveaghtrust.ie
Check website for occasional opening hours. The Museum Flat also opens for special events, such as Open House Dublin
Tara Street DART station (20-min. walk); Luas, Harcourt Street (Green Line, 10-min.walk); Dublin Bus stops 2385 and 2310 are nearby

'It's like Narnia in the wardrobe,' says the man opening the door to No. 3B. And with good reason. During her lifetime, the tiny flat's last tenant, 95-year-old Nellie Molloy, kept the three rooms more or less exactly as they were when her family first arrived in 1915.

The result is like no other museum in the city: a living space frozen in time. At the heart of the sitting room stands an old Lambert range, still set with newspaper for kindling. Above it, there is a brass rail for hanging clothes, with a tasselled yellow drape hiding stove brushes. Lace curtains veil sash windows and quaint, floral wallpaper is bedecked with old family portraits, religious images, crucifixes and various icons like the Infant of Prague. The Iveagh Trust tried to modernise 3B several times (there is no bathroom or running water), but Nellie always refused – preferring her space as her family had kept it and perhaps fearing she might not get it back after a refurbishment. Old crockery remains in the cupboard. Nellie's dresser is peppered with hairclips, perfume and Holy Water. Above it, a little cushion is riddled with clothes pins.

The Iveagh Trust dates from 1890, when it was established by Sir Edward Cecil Guinness to provide affordable housing in Dublin and London. No. 3B was first let in 1904; Nellie's father, a British Army veteran named Henry Molloy, signed his tenancy agreement on 7 June 1915. Nellie and her four siblings slept in one bedroom – boys and girls separated by a curtain hung from a brass rail. Their parents took the other bedroom, sleeping beneath a large shrine to the Virgin Mary whose base Henry had decorated with a brass skirting fashioned from old artillery shells. The stand-up piano in the living room is no ornament – the family loved their hooleys, and wedding breakfasts in the flat were regularly followed by sing-songs.

As a young woman, Nellie worked for a linen company in Harold's Cross, even serving as shop steward before finally leaving to look after her aging mother. She never had a partner or children and, during the 1940s, is said to have declined an offer of marriage from 'a disappointed Kilkenny man'. She died on 29 October 2002, 35 years to the day after her mother. After discussions with her family, the Iveagh Trust purchased the contents of her flat, maintaining it as a museum that grows more magical with every passing year.

GULLIVER'S TRAVELS

Storied figures in stone

Golden Lane & Bride Street,
Dublin 8
Tara Street DART station (15-min. walk); Dublin Bus stop 2383 (2–3-min. walk); Luas, St Stephen's Green (Green Line; 5–10-min. walk)

Jonathan Swift didn't just make his mark on St Patrick's Cathedral. A short distance away from the great building where Swift served as dean from 1713 to 1745, one of his most famous works is celebrated in a series of roundels embedded into the façades of council-built apartments along Golden Lane and Bride Street. Eight separate ceramic disks depict scenes from his classic novel, *Gulliver's Travels*.

As public housing goes, this is some of the best Dublin has to offer. The apartments were built by the then Dublin Corporation in 1998, a sturdy redbrick phalanx garnished with glass block corners, white steel railings and the figurative casts. The roundels followed as the buildings were nearing completion and are the work of Terry Cartin of Cartin Ceramics. Cartin researched the images in the Gilbert Library on Pearse Street before moulding and manipulating the clay, firing it at up to 1,200 degrees, and fitting the pieces together from a cherry picker during a scorching summer ('It was bloody hot,' he recalls). The end results are much loved by residents of the apartments and a creative way of linking this part of Dublin with a great work of satirical literature. Swift's masterpiece was published in 1726 and scenes such as that depicting Gulliver waking to find his arms, legs and hair tied down by the tiny citizens of Lilliput, the giant kissing the queen's hand through her window, or pulling enemy ships with his hands, will be instantly recognisable to anyone who has read the book.

ST PATRICK'S WELL

A subterranean secret in St Patrick's Park

St Patrick's Park, Patrick Street,
Dublin 8
dublincity.ie
Luas, St Stephen's Green (Green Line; 5-min. walk); Dublin Bus stops 2383
and 2385 are nearby on Patrick Street

Very little concrete information exists about the life of St Patrick, but that hasn't stopped stories about the saint cropping up all over Ireland – from sombre sites like Croagh Patrick, where he spent time in the wilderness; or Down Cathedral, where he is reputedly buried; to quirky hits like the Holy Well at Struell, where he is said to have sung psalms all night … while naked.

In Dublin, tradition has it that St Patrick baptised the first Irish Christians in a well – thought to have been located around the site of the present-day St Patrick's Park. Presumably, the saint would have drawn water for his task from the River Poddle, which flows underground today, and a small parish church that stood on an island between two branches of the river was the original St Patrick's. The church was raised to cathedral status in 1213, and remains one of the quintessential Dublin visits today. Both it and the park were the beneficiaries of Guinness largesse, with Sir Benjamin Guinness spending a fortune restoring the cathedral in the 1860s, and Sir Edward Cecil Guinness, Lord Iveagh, developing St Patrick's Park, which was completed in 1904. Within it, in a small bed of shrubs, you'll find a stone plaque indicating that 'near here' was the 'reputed site' of St Patrick's Well.

This isn't just fanciful thinking. In 1901 building works beside the cathedral unearthed six Celtic grave slabs. Subsequently dated to the 10th century, one of the granite slabs seems to have covered the remains of an ancient well. Two can be seen inside the cathedral today, where a plaque dates them to between 800 and 1100. The stone on the left is the one to look out for, resting on a plinth that declares it to have been found six feet [1.28m] below the surface on the traditional site of St Patrick's Well. Sadly, there is no information as to whether the saint was naked on his visit.

THE COOMBE MONUMENT

Dublin characters, cast in stone

The Coombe,
Dublin 8
Dublin Bus stop 5025; Luas, Harcourt Street (Green Line; 15-min. walk)

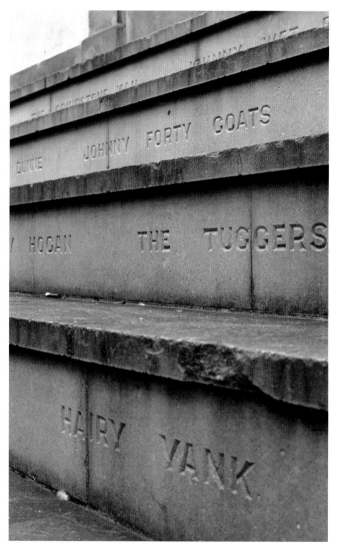

Towards the end of 1825, two women and their newborn babies perished in heavy snow while attempting to reach the Rotunda Hospital. When their heart-wrenching story became public knowledge, a number of 'benevolent and well-disposed people' clubbed together to found the Coombe Lying-In (Maternity) Hospital for the relief of poor women. History was made.

So we learn from the plaque affixed to this Dublin monument – a striking portico that looks like it's been beamed down next to a housing development along the Coombe. In fact, it's the other way round – the portico pre-dates the housing development and it served as the entrance to the Coombe Hospital until the institution moved to its present-day location in Dolphin's Barn in 1967. Although the hospital itself dates back to 1770, the maternity service for which it's known wasn't founded until 1826, when £100 was donated in memory of those two unfortunate Dublin mothers. After its relocation, the old hospital building was demolished to make way for today's modern redbrick development, with the granite portico restored by Dublin Corporation as a memorial to mothers who gave birth 'to future citizens of Ireland' at the hospital, as well as to its staff and friends.

Those citizens have been a colourful bunch, if the steps to the rear of the portico are anything to judge by. Look closely and you'll see the names of several local characters inscribed in the stone: men like P. J. 'Johnny Forty Coats' Marlow (who wore three or four overcoats no matter what the weather), Skin the Rasher, Shell Shock Joe, The Tuggers, the Hairy Yank, Lady Hogan, the Prince of Denmark, the Earl of Dalcashin, Bugler Dunner, Jembo No Toes and perhaps most beloved of all – Thomas 'Bang Bang' Dudley.

Bang Bang's nickname stems from the mock shoot-outs he staged with his 'gun' – a large church key. He was a lifelong fan of cowboy movies and locals regularly humoured him by returning fire on the streets. 'Despite progressive eye disease, Bang Bang maintained his daily beat in the city, frequently causing mayhem by jumping onto buses, slapping his rear end as if he was on a horse,' the *Irish Independent*'s obituary reported after his death in 1989.

RUSH LAMP

The light of Dean Swift's life ...

St Patrick's Cathedral, St Patrick's Close,
Dublin 8
01 453-9472
stpatrickscathedral.ie
March–October: Monday–Friday 9am–5.30pm, Saturday 9am–6.30pm,
Sunday 9am–11am, 1pm–3pm & 4.30pm–6.30pm; November–February:
Monday–Friday 9.30am–5pm, Saturday 9am–5.30pm, Sunday 9am–11am
& 1pm–3pm
Luas (Green Line) (5–10-min. walk from St Stephen's Green); Dublin Buses
49, 54a, 27, 56a, 77a and 150 all stop next to St Patrick's Cathedral

There are many mementos of Jonathan Swift at St Patrick's Cathedral. Swift famously served as dean here from 1713 until his death in 1745, and along with the pulpit from which he preached, visitors can see two rather pointy-nosed death masks, Swift's grave, a cast of his skull and a table at which he celebrated the Eucharist in his country parish in Co. Meath. Given his reputation as a writer, it's not surprising to find the cathedral in possession of some early editions, too.

Swift was almost 78 when he died, a ridiculously old age for the time, leading to speculation that his penchant for exercise and cleanliness may have paid a healthy dividend. 'At a time when people rarely washed, Swift was obsessed with cleanliness,' we are told. 'He also exercised every day. In pleasant weather, he walked or went horseback riding. When bad weather kept him inside, Swift raced up and down the three sets of stairs in the Deanery.' Talk about being ahead of the curve.

The most evocative artefact of all, however, is one of the least remarked upon. You'll find it in the cabinet alongside his waxy death mask – it's a rush lamp, by the light of which Swift and his closest friend, Esther Johnson (known as Stella), are said to have read together. At the time, rush lamps were regarded as lights for the poor – their flames coaxed from reeds soaked in flammable substances, such as wax, rather than more expensive candles. Swift never married, and scholars have debated the exact nature of his relationship with his muse, but he clearly delighted in Stella's company, writing to her daily when he was away in London, and composing ditties too. 'Since I first saw thee at 16/ The brightest virgin on the green/So little is thy form declined/Made up so largely in thy mind,' as he wrote on her 34th birthday. The affection was repaid – Stella, who first met Swift when he worked for Sir William Temple on his estate in Surrey, moved to Ireland to be nearer the dean.

Whatever the nature of their relationship, there's something irresistibly romantic about this little rush lamp. Can't you imagine the pair huddled up together in a cavernous cathedral interior? Stella died, aged just 46, in 1728 (we are not privy to her exercise regime). Overcome with grief, Swift moved out of his usual rooms to avoid seeing her funeral lights in the cathedral windows.

MARSH'S LIBRARY

Ireland's first public library

St Patrick's Close, Dublin 8
01 454-3511
marshlibrary.ie
Tuesday–Friday 9.30am–5pm; Saturday: 10am–5pm
Reading room by appointment only
Luas (Green Line) (5–10-min. walk from St Stephen's Green); Dublin Buses
49, 54a, 27, 56a, 77a and 150 all stop next to St Patrick's Cathedral

It may be Ireland's first public library, but there's a sizeable portion of Dubliners who have never heard of – let alone visited – the squirrelled-away Marsh's Library on St Patrick's Close.

The library is named after Archbishop Narcissus March (1638–1713), under whom it was built in 1701. Designed by Sir William Robinson, the architect responsible for the Royal Hospital at Kilmainham, its collection of 25,000 books is a picture-perfect example of how a fusty old library should be. Step through the ivy-strewn entrance arch, mosey up the dank steps, ring the bell and finally you are ushered into the hushed interior. Pay €5 to the gatekeeper and allow your eyes a moment to adjust to the rich palette of browns: the oak bookcases, the lettered gables, the beautifully tactile leather-bound books themselves. It feels like the kind of room in which you might stumble upon a lost literary secret, an ancient cure or the beginnings of a murder mystery (some of the books even bear bullet holes from the 1916 Easter Rising).

The books themselves date largely from the 16th to the 18th centuries and cover religion, medicine, law, travel, science, mathematics, music and classical literature. They range from hefty tomes to tiny curiosities: a small collection of verse, for instance, contains a poem to Queen Elizabeth I by Sir Walter Raleigh. Marsh's Library also contains some 300 manuscripts, with one 'Lives of the Irish Saints' dating from 1400, and a Hebrew tome printed in 1491 bearing a note in the archbishop's own hand: '*Liber rarissimus*' (rare book). There are even special 'cages' interspersed with the bookshelves – in times gone by, readers were locked into them while perusing rare books.

This is more than just a collection of old books, however. 'Please try me!' reads a note in a ledger, inviting visitors to try the collection of quills. There's a death mask of Jonathan Swift and a skull cast of his friend and muse, Stella. Regular exhibitions based around themes in the books open up whole worlds of mystery and delight – such as the amazingly random 'Anatomical Account of the Elephant Accidentally Burnt in Dublin on Friday, June 17, in the Year 1681'. Who knew?

Among the relics, you may stumble across Narcissus Marsh himself. As the story goes, the archbishop was distraught when his niece, Grace, ran away to marry in secret. Grace wrote a letter to her uncle, which she stashed in the pages of one of his books, but Marsh was reportedly never able to locate it.

To this day, his ghost continues the search …

THE CABBAGE GARDENS

(32)

'Think of God and follow me'

Cathedral Lane, off Kevin Street, Dublin 8
dublincity.ie
Daily: December & January: 10am–5pm; February & November: 10am–
5.30pm; March & October: 10am–6.30pm; April & September: 10am–
8.30pm; May & August: 10am–9.30pm; June & July: 10am–10pm
Admission: free
Dublin Bus stop 2311 is nearby on Kevin Street Upper: it's served by the 150,
151, 27, 26a and 77a bus routes; Luas, Harcourt St (Green Line; 10-min.
walk)

Despite the earthy title, this is not the place to come for a head of cabbage.

Located at the top of Cathedral Lane, the Cabbage Gardens are in fact a small park named for the fact that Oliver Cromwell and his soldiers are said to have cultivated the vegetables here after their arrival on these shores in 1649. Cabbages hadn't been grown in Ireland before this time, so they must have seemed pretty exotic (Cathedral Lane itself was known as Cabbage Garden Lane until 1792). Today, however, you'll find a lung of green space surrounded by stacked gravestones, council flats and a five-a-side pitch.

The gravestones came after the cabbages – they date back to 1666, when the gardens were granted as a cemetery to the Parish of St Nicholas Without by the Dean and Chapter of St Patrick's Cathedral. Many local parishioners were buried there (as an information sign explains), including shoemakers, clothiers, grocers and timber merchants. In 1681 they were joined by French Huguenots, who leased a narrow strip of land in the north-western corner of the gardens. One of the most famous is David Digues La Touche des Rompières, who founded La Touche Bank – the precursor of today's Bank of Ireland – with fellow weaver Nathaniel Kane in 1722. He was buried here in 1745. Although Dublin City Council moved dozens of gravestones to the edge of the park when they opened it to the public in 1982, many inscriptions are still clearly legible today. A headstone erected by Henry Medcalfe 'of the Poddle' in memory of his 20-year-old son John, for example, carries the jolly reminder:

Passengers as you pass by
As you are now so once was I
As I am now so shall you be
Think of God and follow me

Sadly, judging by the deteriorating state of the headstones, such messages may not be visible for much longer. Memorials in the north-western corner in particular have been thrashed by vandals, leaving their stone breaking apart, their inscriptions crumbling and their legacies collapsing into gravel littered with broken glass and cigarette butts.

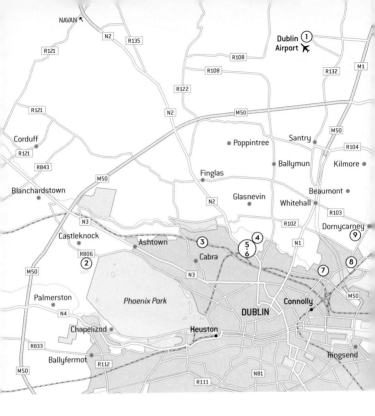

Outside the Centre – North

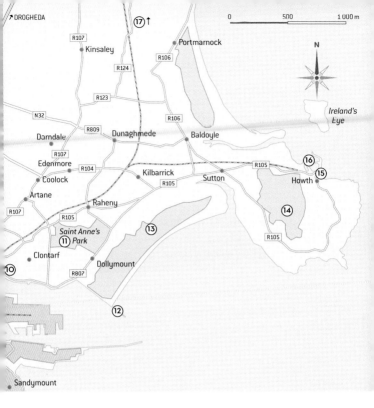

OLD TERMINAL BUILDING

The golden age of Irish air travel

Dublin Airport, Co. Dublin
dublinairport.com
The old terminal opens occasionally for tours, such as during Open
House Dublin, the Irish Architecture Foundation's annual open day
(openhousedublin.com)
Dublin Bus routes 16 and 41 connect the airport and city, as do several
private coach services

Dublin Airport officially opened for business on 19 January 1940, when a propeller-driven Aer Lingus Lockheed 14 departed for Liverpool on a chilly Thursday morning.

Since then, the airport has mushroomed into a sprawling complex capable of processing 30 million passengers a year. The original building has been swallowed up in a spaghetti of terminals, runways, taxiways, access roads and office buildings, but passengers walking the skybridge between Terminal 1 and Pier D can steal a glimpse at the toothpaste-white façade and surgically curvy architecture in all their nostalgic glory. Surprisingly, the modernist jewel remains a working building, housing

DAA offices, the Met Office's airport presence and some passenger boarding gates – so it's effectively still in use as a terminal.

Work on the building began in the late 1930s, to a design by Desmond FitzGerald. The tiered floors echo the form of a great ocean liner, and the building's form curved deliberately to present a long façade towards taxiing aircraft, and a shorter concave to arriving passengers – seeming to embrace them as they arrived at the door. Inside, check-in desks faced out into a double-height foyer, visitors were free to access the balconies as a viewing platform, and the staircase, with its travertine steps and brass railings, survives. The same cannot be said, alas, for a restaurant (run by the legendary Johnny Opperman) that once looked out onto the airfield, or the dances held here at night – something almost impossible to imagine today. But then, this was a time of handwritten tickets, going-away suits and security-free zones; a golden age of air travel immortalised on Dublin Airport's Pinterest site (pinterest.com/dublinairport). When Dublin's first transatlantic flight took off in 1958, Eamon de Valera quoted Charles Lindbergh· 'In any development of transatlantic travel, Ireland holds the key.'

Of course, it wasn't all romance. Air travel was notoriously expensive before the days of budget airlines, and many of those passing through this beautiful Old Terminal Building would have been emigrating – some never to return. Over time, Dublin's trickle of flights became a flood. Built to accommodate just 100,000 passengers a year, the original building was well and truly outgrown by the late 1950s, when a new North Terminal was added.

DUNSINK OBSERVATORY

That pot of gold under a dump

Castleknock, Dublin 15
dunsink.dias.ie
Free public events and visitor nights run several times in winter
*Travel by bike or car is recommended – if travelling by Dublin bus (38) there
is a 1.5-km walk up Dunsink Lane*

Driving deep into the suburbs of Castleknock, you mightn't expect
to find the oldest purpose-built scientific research centre in Ireland.
But that's exactly what Dunsink Observatory is.

Dating from 1785, when it opened as a facility for Trinity College,
Dunsink is best known as the workplace of the great William Rowan
Hamilton (1805–65), but it has its quirkier stories too.

The observatory is today part of the Dublin Institute for Advanced
Studies, and although not open to the public per se, it is used for public
outreach – hosting events during Science Week in November, for
example, Culture Night in September, Open House in October, or open
nights supported by the Irish Astronomical Society (irishastrosoc.org).
These tend to include talks, Q&As and, weather permitting, the chance
to gaze through the historic Grubb Telescope in the South Dome –
it dates from 1868, a time when the Rathmines firm was exporting
telescopes all over the world.

Inside the house itself, a line-up of old clocks evokes the observatory's
former role in setting Ireland's time standard (some 25 minutes and 21
seconds behind GMT).

Nixon's 'goodwill moon rocks'

If you do attend a talk, you might ask how a lunar rock reportedly worth up to €4 million ended up in the nearby rubbish dump. The story dates back to Richard Nixon's presidency, when hundreds of moon rocks were sent as gifts around the world following the final Apollo landing expedition. Ireland's was kept in Dunsink Observatory, but got lost following a fire on 3 October 1977. In an interview with the BBC, a scientist who worked at Dunsink at the time claimed that the rock had been deposited with the rest of the rubble into Dunsink landfill nearby. 'That pot of gold under a dump' is how Joseph Gutheinz Jr, a Texas-based lawyer and former NASA agent, described it to the BBC.

Finding the pea-sized treasure would be almost impossible, of course, but Dubliners can take some comfort in the fact that they are not alone – almost half of Nixon's 'goodwill moon rocks' are said to be unaccounted for.

BROOME BRIDGE

An equation etched in stone

Broombridge Station, Cabra, Dublin 7
Dublin Bus stops 286 and 828 are nearby on Carnlough Road; Broombridge
station is about 10 min. by Commuter service from Connolly station

On 16 October 1843, Sir William Rowan Hamilton was struck by 'a flash of genius' while walking along the banks of the Royal Canal. In that moment, as commemorated by a plaque on Broome Bridge, the physicist, astronomer and mathematician conceived of the fundamental formula for quaternion multiplication 'and cut it on a stone of this bridge'.

Archimedes had his 'Eureka' moment in the bath. Hamilton (1805–65) had his while out walking with his wife. For years, the Dubliner had been pondering how to extend complex numbers to three dimensions, but suddenly he struck upon the idea of using four dimensions instead. 'A very curious train of mathematical speculation occurred to me,' as he wrote in a letter the following day. Pulling out a pocketknife, Hamilton cut his formula into the stone:

$$i^2 + j^2 + k^2 = ijk = -1$$

In 1958 a memorial plaque was unveiled by Éamon de Valera, himself a keen mathematician who had spent hours as a young man scouring the bridge for evidence of the equation. His search was in vain. 'The weather had done its work,' as Prof. Annraoí de Paor of UCD, who was present at the unveiling, recalls in his essay 'An Unworldly Scholar'.

Quaternions, four-dimensional numbers to which the commutative law of multiplication does not apply, blew algebra wide open. Hamilton's discovery paved the way for several major scientific breakthroughs, including the development of vector analysis and the theory of electromagnetic waves. Even today, as a mathematical shorthand for rotation calculations in 4D, quaternions are central to movie special effects, the control of spacecraft and computer graphics – they were used to create Lara Croft in the computer game, 'Tomb Raider', for example. But Hamilton didn't stop there. He also invented biquaternions, made major contributions in mechanics, optics and geometry, and was knighted in 1835.

Sadly, Broome Bridge is not such an inspiring setting today. Sandwiched between a railway station and an industrial estate, its stony hump is regularly festooned with litter and graffiti and brightened only by the occasional duck or swan. A Hamilton walk is held annually on 16 October, however, setting out from his former base at Dunsink Observatory.

WITTGENSTEIN'S STEP

'When the sun shines in my brain ...'

National Botanic Gardens, Glasnevin, Dublin 9
01 857-0909 (visitor centre)
botanicgardens.ie
Winter: Monday–Friday 9am–4.30pm, weekends & public holidays
10am–4.30pm
Summer: Monday–Friday 9am–5pm, weekends & public holidays
10am–6pm
Admission: free
Dublin Bus routes 4 and 9 (from O'Connell Street) and 83 (Kimmage/
Harristown)

The National Botanic Gardens are home to some 17,000 plant species, but just as exotic is this modest bronze plaque found in its Victorian palm house. It marks the spot (or step, to be precise) where Ludwig Wittgenstein (1889–1951) came to sit and write in his notebook during a short but very productive stay in Dublin over the course of a winter in the late 1940s.

During his stay, the Viennese philosopher roomed at the Ross Hotel on Parkgate Street. He is said to have liked Dublin – describing it as having the air of 'a real capital city' – and during the winter of 1948 he spent time writing, thinking, walking, enjoying black coffee and omelettes at Bewley's of Grafton Street and relaxing with his good friend, the Irish physicist Dr Con Drury, according to Richard Wall's book, *Wittgenstein in Dublin* (Reaktion Books, 2000). His stay appears to have been fruitful, too. 'When I came here I found to my surprise that I could work again; and as I'm anxious to make hay during the very short period when the sun shines in my brain, I've decided … to stay here where I've got a warm and quiet room,' the philosopher wrote in a letter dated 6 November 1948. Wittgenstein was troubled by health issues that winter, but not enough to prevent regular visits to the National Botanic Gardens, whose Victorian palm house may have reminded him of Vienna. Sitting inside this lovely spaceship of a structure, he would have been insulated from the chilly weather, and it's tempting to imagine him working on his posthumously published work, *Philosophical Investigations* (1953). Strangely for an author seen by many as the greatest philosopher of the 20th century, Wittgenstein only had a single book – the 75-page *Tractatus Logico-Philosophicus* – published during his lifetime.

The National Botanic Gardens, which date from 1795, are home to Ireland's richest plant collection. Over 300 of its specimens are rare or endangered, with six technically extinct in the wild. The palm house was erected in 1883 after a previous structure was damaged in a storm.

DANIEL O'CONNELL'S CRYPT

'My body to Ireland, my soul to heaven, my heart to Rome'

Glasnevin Cemetery, Finglas Road, Dublin 11
01 882-6500
dctrust.ie
8am–6pm; tour only accessible via scheduled tours
A Tower Tour ticket gives combined access to the crypt and tower (over 8s only; visitors need 'a reasonable level of fitness' to climb the steps)
Dublin Bus 140 from O'Connell Street

A 52m-tall granite tower marking the burial place of Daniel O'Connell (1775–1847) dominates Glasnevin Cemetery. It's impossible to avoid George Petrie's monument when you enter the cemetery gates – indeed, as the highest round tower in Ireland, the structure is visible for several kilometres around. Since 2018, visitors have once again been able to scale the 198 steps to one of the best 360-degree views in the city, but don't be tempted to rush to the top. The crypt beneath this soaring structure will arguably leave a deeper impression.

O'Connell's last resting place was restored prior to recent work on the tower and its staircase (for years, it had been cut off with concrete blocks) and features a Kilkenny marble altar inscribed with a Durrow Cross as its centrepiece. The tomb is contained within a room decorated with a swirling mix of Christian and Celtic symbols, a mosaic-tiled floor and a sculpted scene of the Crucifixion. Also featured, in gold lettering on a green band, is O'Connell's dying wish: 'My body to Ireland, my soul to heaven, my heart to Rome.'

The Liberator died in Genoa while on a pilgrimage to the Italian capital, and in accordance with his wishes, his heart continued on to the Irish College in Rome while his body was interred at Glasnevin. Strangely, the oak and lead-lined coffin lies within easy reach through several shamrock-shaped holes in the stone. It's said that touching it brings the visitor luck, and around the edges that are easiest to access, the wood has been worn smooth. If you bend down and peer right into the recesses, a cross and inscription can be made out, covered in a layer of dust. The closeness feels extraordinary – especially when you recall that the monument was the target of a suspected loyalist bomb attack in the 1970s … the reason for the tower's decades of closure.

O'Connell, renowned for his success in securing Catholic Emancipation, was also responsible for the establishment of the non-denominational Glasnevin Cemetery in 1832. At the time, Irish Catholics had no dedicated cemeteries of their own, and the lands were acquired to lay to rest 'people of all religion and none'. Several members of O'Connell's family have also been interred beneath the tower – somewhat unsettlingly, their wooden coffins can be seen stacked on top of each other in a little room branching off the main crypt.

MICHAEL COLLINS' SECRET ADMIRER

The Big Fella's blooms …

Glasnevin Cemetery, Finglas Road, Dublin 11
dctrust.ie
Monday–Sunday 8am–6pm
Dublin Bus route 140 departs from O'Connell Street

Some 1.2 million souls are buried at Glasnevin Cemetery, ranging from political leaders like Daniel O'Connell, Charles Stewart Parnell and Éamon de Valera to nameless victims of Ireland's famine and cholera outbreaks. For sheer star power, however, none can match the cult of Michael Collins (1890–1922) – his is Glasnevin's most visited grave.

Set just behind the cemetery's distinctive museum and cafe, the grave and cross are often bedecked with pops of flowers that seem to refresh themselves on a daily basis. 'It's got nothing to do with us', a guide told Secret Dublin on one visit, describing the procession of visitors bearing blooms, cards and even love letters to the last resting place of the charismatic hero, who was assassinated at the age of 32. Some of the fresh flowers are sent or personally delivered, he revealed, by a mysterious French lady. 'I think her name is Véronique.'

Indeed it is. *The Sunday Independent* identified Véronique Crombé, a museum guide and lecturer from Paris, as Collins' secret admirer. In an interview with the newspaper, Crombé described the 'overwhelming' desire she has to keep his memory alive – a desire sparked when she first saw Neil Jordan's movie, *Michael Collins* (1996). On 22 August 2000, the anniversary of Collins' death at Béal na Bláth, Crombé felt the inexplicable need to rush into a cathedral to light a candle. 'The 22nd, the date he was shot dead, was the decisive moment which helped me understand that definitely, sooner or later, I would have to go to Ireland to know more and that going to his grave would show me the way. That Michael himself was drawing me to continue on his story.' Her first visit to Glasnevin had a profound effect, she says. 'It was the start of something that is still with me. When a person dies young, an energy is left behind. An energy surrounding things left undone.'

Crombé still sends flowers on significant anniversaries (she travelled to Ireland for the 100th anniversary of Collins' death in 2022). But she's not alone in her devotion. For years, the Big Fella's grave had been looked after by another admirer, Dennis Lenihan. Several other men, united by a similar passion and interest, joined him – including James Langton, Paul Callery, Ronnie Daly, Paul Fleming and Rod Dennison. The Collins 22 society tends the grave and lays flowers. The 'mysterious French lady' has a romantic appeal, Véronique concedes, but she urges us not to forget the dedication of her friends.

JEWISH CEMETERY

Built in the year 5618

67 Fairview Strand, Ballybough, Dublin 3
dublincity.ie
Open by appointment only
Clontarf Road DART station (10 to 15-min walk); Dublin Bus 123 stops at
bus stop 4518 on Fairview Strand at Richmond Road

'**B**uilt in the year 5618'. If ever a plaque was designed to grab your attention, this is it. Even its context is mystifying. It's set into the wall of a tiny gatehouse that looks ready to float off at any moment, like Mr Fredricksen's house in the film *Up*. What's the story?

First off, don't worry. Fairview Strand is not a blip in the space-time continuum: 5618 is a date from the Hebrew calendar, which is based on lunar months. The equivalent year in the Gregorian calendar is 1857, when the lodge was constructed. And beyond it lies Fairview's Jewish cemetery.

The cemetery itself dates from 1718, when it was leased from Captain Chichester Phillips of Drumcondra Castle. It was bought outright in 1748, 'as a leasehold for 1,000 years at the annual rent of one peppercorn', as Diarmuid G. Hiney writes in the *Dublin Historical Record* (Vol. 50, No. 2, 1997), and served as a burial ground for Jews living in Dublin until 1900, when a larger cemetery opened in Dolphin's Barn. The last burial took place here in 1958.

Though the area can feel run-down today, Fairview Strand was once a fashionable place with fine views of Dublin Bay. The lodge, or mortuary house, was built to house a caretaker. High walls were added for greater privacy and to protect against grave-robbers – a scourge of Dublin cemeteries at the time. 'In 1839, laws of the Dublin Jewish Congregation stated that after every burial, bodies should be watched for a week', Hiney writes. 'A quaint anecdote is told about the headstone of Solomon Cohen which disappeared, and one of his sons on visiting a Christian friend in the area, noted that his father was buried in the chimney breast.' One wonders if Mr Cohen's remains still lie in the listed building ...

More recently, Dublin City Council took the site over from the Dublin Jewish Board of Guardians. Although it had become dilapidated, on Secret Dublin's latest visit it was being restored, with future plans to open it to the public. Today's lodge door and window frames are a striking black, but not long ago the sole window above the '5618' plaque was spotted with Catholic icons like the Infant of Prague, the Virgin Mary and St Anthony ... complete with lace curtain. If curiosity gets the better of you, take a seat upstairs on the No.123 double-decker bus. It passes right by the historic cemetery; you may be able to peer over the wall.

'SPITE ROW'

Bram Stoker's birthplace

Marino Crescent, Clontarf, Dublin 3
Clontarf Road DART station (2 to 3-min walk); bus stop 613 is nearby on
Howth Road, beside Marino Crescent

Why is the handsome, curving Marino Crescent also known as 'Spite Row'? The answer stems from the nearby Casino at Marino – whose views over Dublin Bay were likened by its owner, Lord Charlemont, to the Bay of Naples (he went so far as to build servants' tunnels so their comings and goings wouldn't spoil it). When a developer named Charlie Ffolliott announced plans to build homes between the Casino and the sea, the Earl was disgusted – and levied heavy tolls on building materials brought over his land. Ffolliott brought the materials by barge instead, and took his revenge by having Marino Crescent, completed in 1792, work partly like a screen obstructing the Casino's vistas.

What's more, Ffolliott is said to have built the back of the terrace – the side facing Marino House (Lord Charlemont's principal residence, also located nearby) – in a deliberately higgledy-piggledy style to maximise the ugly factor, the *Irish Independent* reported when one of the houses came up for sale recently. 'The two adjoining tallest houses in the terrace were cranked up specifically to clobber the view from the living room windows of Marino House.'

Visit the Crescent today and you'll find a leafy residential street curving round the oval Bram Stoker Park. It's named after the author of *Dracula*, who was born on the Georgian terrace. Bram was born in 1847 to Abraham Stoker and Charlotte Mathilda Blake Thornley, who lived at No.15 – a slim, three-storey-over-basement affair that remains a private house today. The third of seven children, Stoker was a sickly child and lay bedridden with a mystery illness until he was 7. 'I was naturally thoughtful, and the leisure of long illness gave opportunity for many thoughts which were fruitful according to their kind in later years', he would write. During these early years, could his mother have begun passing on horror stories of cholera victims buried alive in her native Sligo? It's tempting to think so ... 'Spite Row' could as just easily be called 'Bite Row'.

The strange case of the Russian crown jewels

No.15 didn't just hide the secrets of Dracula. Also associated with family members of IRB member Harry Boland (1887–1922), for decades it was the hiding place of several Russian crown jewels, which had been given to Ireland by Lenin's new government as security for a loan in 1920. In the tumult of the Civil War, Boland had asked his family to keep them until an Irish Republic had been established. In 1937, when the Constitution was enacted, they followed his instruction, and the jewels were eventually returned to Russia.

CASINO AT MARINO

A small house with a big reputation ...

Cherrymount Crescent, off Malahide Road, Marino, Dublin 3
heritageireland.ie
10am–5.30pm (last tour at 4pm)
Clontarf Dart Station (15-min walk); Dublin Bus routes 14, 27, 27a, 27b, 128
(from Eden Quay), and 42, 43 (from Abbey St Lower) stop at Bus Stop No.
665 on Malahide Road

I t's Dublin's littlest big house. Or perhaps its biggest little house.
Designed by Sir William Chambers as a flight of fancy for James

Caulfield, the First Earl of Charlemont, the Casino at Marino at first looks like it could be an estate folly.

'You would think it's a one-storey neoclassical building', as the OPW guide said on Secret Dublin's visit. 'But is it? It's all about deception and trickery, this building.'

Despite having only a handful of visible windows, the Casino (from the Italian for 'small house') actually contains 16 rooms. Not only that, they're breathtakingly rich in subtlety and design. Here is 'one of the most fascinating essays in stone in Ireland', as David Newman Johnson wrote in the *Irish Arts Review*. Details like the plasterwork, with its intricate rows of eggs, acorns or Greek keys, or inlaid floors and curved mahogany doors, are astonishing. Ditto the stateroom on a third floor invisible from without, or a tiny 'Zodiac Room' whose domed ceiling is an optical illusion making it hard to tell the actual height.

Lord Charlemont's inspiration came from his Grand Tour of Europe. It was fashionable at the time to adorn estates with garden temples, hunting lodges, hermitages and the like – but the Casino, begun in 1760 and completed over two decades on his Marino estate, was a more unusual miniature. Its principal floor takes the form of a Greek cross, surrounded by a dozen or so Doric columns. Its Portland stone carvings are beautifully rendered, the rooftop urns mask a pair of chimneys, and inside – another surprise – there are two storeys and a basement, containing eight vaulted servants' rooms. In the saloon, guests were served dishes like turtle soup, flambéed badger and fashionable pineapples (look for them in the plasterwork, too). The depth of detailing throughout ensures that, 250 years on, the Casino is regarded as one of the most exquisite neo-classical garden temples in Europe, and an hour is quickly swallowed up on a tour.

And that's not even starting on the tunnels sprawling under the lawns. These are the subject of all sorts of local legends, with some insiting they once stretched to the Wicklow Mountains and the Hellfire Club. The tour does reveal, however, that Michael Collins and his men practised shooting a Thompson ('Tommy') sub-machine gun in one of the tunnels in 1921. Several ricochet marks can even be seen on the walls opposite the entrance.

© OPWD18872-0017

ST ANTHONY'S HALL

Birthplace of the nation?

Clontarf Road, Dublin 3
01 833-3459
stanthonysclontarf.ie
Clontarf DART station (10-min. walk); Dublin Bus routes 130 and 32x stop
at bus stops 1737 and 1742 on Clontarf Road

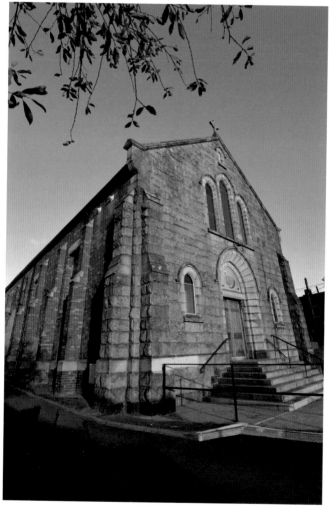

Where exactly is the birthplace of the modern Irish nation? The GPO, where Padraig Pearse read the Proclamation of the Republic in April 1916? Kilmainham Gaol, where the leaders of that Rising were executed? The Shelbourne Hotel, where the constitution was drafted in 1922?

Or perhaps somewhere rather less grandiose. Say, a town hall in Clontarf?

At first glance, St Anthony's Hall appears more like a church. Indeed, this was its function for several decades before the present-day parish church (to the rear) was built in 1975. Prior to 1925, however, it served as a town hall and was let out by Dublin Corporation for various purposes – concerts, movies, dances and the like. One of those events was held to raise money for Peadar Kearney, author of the national anthem, after he shot himself in the foot during rifle practice with the Irish Republican Brotherhood's Dublin Brigade.

Members of the IRB also used the space to congregate for some years, with a key meeting held on Sunday, 16 January 1916. Behind closed doors that evening, the Supreme Council of the IRB made a decision that was to change the course of Irish history – albeit unbeknownst to many of those present. The military council had been edging towards setting Easter Sunday as a date for a rising in the city, and at this meeting, Sean McDermott moved that the IRB should rise 'at the earliest possible time'. One of those present 'recalled [Padraig] Pearse hinting about Easter, and somebody replying that it was a busy time for farmers,' as Austen Ogran writes in his biography of James Connolly. 'The Supreme Council assented in ignorance of the plans for Easter Sunday.' History was made.

In 1998, alas, a substantial portion of the former town hall was demolished – including the historic room where the IRB decided to authorise the Easter Rising.

Two years before the Easter Rising, Clontarf had been the location for another skirmish that might well have influenced the course of history. In 1914 Volunteers running guns from Howth were intercepted at Clontarf by a force of police and soldiers. 'A parley took place,' as Michael Collins told the author Hayden Talbot. Shots were fired, and one of the Volunteers was bayoneted.

'By this time there was only the front rank of our force anywhere in sight! The rest of us … had disappeared across the fields! And so not one gun was lost!'

FOLLIES OF ST ANNE'S PARK

The last demesne landscape in the city

St Anne's Park, Clontarf
dublincity.ie
10am until dark (5pm–10pm, depending on the time of year)
Admission: free
Dublin Buses 29a and 130 connect the city centre to St Anne's Park, stopping next to the entrance on Mount Prospect Avenue

An 11m-tall 'Roman tower' that once stood on the roof of a Guinness family mansion. A 'Pompeiian temple' formerly used as a teahouse. A 'hermit's cave' carved into an ornamental bridge. Sham ruins, a clock tower with a 1.2m-high bell that still rings out over Clontarf and, perhaps most evocatively, a 'Shell House' once used to house an exotic fern collection. Walkers will find the woods, playing fields and water features of St Anne's Park full of surprises, and though many locals are aware of these structures, few realise their number, or the reason why they are there.

The answer? These are follies dating from the 19th century, when St Anne's Park was a demesne owned by the Guinness family. In Victorian times, it was the fashion for mind-bogglingly rich aristocrats to decorate their lands with romantic reminders of 'Grand Tours' in Europe. Given the wealth at their disposal, the family (who also owned Ashford Castle) didn't do things by halves. Sir Benjamin Lee Guinness, and subsequently Lord and Lady Ardilaun, were responsible for the landscaping of the park around their North Dublin mansion (sadly destroyed by fire in 1943).

The Shell House, similar to another Irish example at Carton House in Co. Kildare, was a fashionable fancy at a time when 'shellwork' was a hobby for ladies. Queen Victoria passed beneath one of the sham ruins, a turreted bridge, when she called at Clontarf during a state visit to Ireland in 1900. A circular yew hedge surrounding a marble basin was once peppered with allegorical statues representing the continents. Though radically reduced in size, this sprawling green lung still forms 'the last remaining example of an Irish demesne landscape in the capital city', as Maryann Harris, Senior Executive Parks Superintendent, wrote in a study for Dublin City Council in 2009.

Today, St Anne's Park – which takes its name from a holy well (now dry) near the pond – knits together woodland walks, playing pitches, model gardens and long, straight avenues as well as a restaurant and farmers' market in the mansion's former red stables. Thankfully, after years struggling with disrepair, overgrowth and vandalisation, the Guinness follies have been conserved by the Dublin City Council Parks Department. The old surprises are getting a new lease of life, though unfortunately the Shell House, housed in a park nursery and depot works area, will not be open to the public.

REALT NA MARA

Star of the sea

Bull Island, Clontarf, County Dublin
Dart (Clontarf Road Dart Station, 30-min walk); Dublin Bus stops 1751
and 1727 are nearby on Clontarf Road, serviced by the 130 bus from Lower
Abbey Street

I n 1950, Dublin dockers began paying instalments of a shilling into a fund created for the construction of a memorial to Our Lady in Dublin Bay. When a guinea (21 shillings) had been amassed, they were issued with a signed certificate: a document that hung proudly in many houses.

Delays finding a site meant that their monument – Clontarf's soaring 'Realt na Mara' ('Star of the Sea') – wasn't unveiled until 1972. But all those thousands of shillings were put to good use in the end.

Set at the end of the North Bull Wall, reached after crossing Bull Island's iconic single-lane wooden bridge, the walk out to 'Realt na Mara' is as nostalgic as it is bracing. Along the way, you'll pass bathing areas and may spot kite-surfers and exotic birds hovering over Dollymount Strand (sometimes, it's hard to distinguish between the two). Our Lady herself lies at the walk's endpoint, a windy spot where views extend to Howth and Bray Head. Perched 70-foot atop of a concrete tripod, the bronze statue, which was sculpted by Cecil King, watches over Dublin Bay – hands turned outwards, palms upwards. She is borne aloft by three pillars of Connemara marble, and 12 cut-glass stars were later added to her halo, donated by Waterford Crystal. You might spot them glistening in the sun, or seeming to sparkle as they reflect light from the floodlights below.

Even without the Catholic context, the sense of an angel watching over the water feels strangely comforting. And indeed, one of the main committee members involved in bringing Realt na Mara to the city – William Nelson, a sailor whose coal ship came under attack from a German U-boat in 1917 – said he was inspired by his devotion to Our Lady, who he felt watched over him. 'He was determined to get the statue erected so it would watch over and protect Dublin Port workers and seafarers', his grandson Bill Nelson told the *Irish Independent* on the statue's 50th anniversary in 2022.

BIRDS OF BULL ISLAND

One reason Dublin Bay is today a UNESCO Biosphere Reserve

Clontarf, County Dublin
bullislandbirds.com; birdwatchireland.ie
Access Bull Island via the wooden bridge at Clontarf, or further north via the causeway road; Dublin Bus route 130 stops at the wooden bridge (stops 1727 and 1572). You can park along the Causeway, which is also about 1.2 km from Raheny Dart Station

© Fáilte Ireland / Gareth McCormack

Bull Island is just a baby. Before the completion of Dublin's Great South Wall in 1795, and North Bull Wall in 1824, it didn't exist.

Afterwards, the walls caused deposits of sand and silt to pile up at the North Bull. Bit by bit, the island has grown into a billowy, sandy, grassy oasis that looks like it has been in Dublin Bay forever. Today stretching some 5 km long, visitors can enjoy it in various ways, from swims and kitesurfing on the expansive Dollymount Strand (where many locals learned to drive) to walking its dunes, causeways and sands. Following various trails here, you could potter about for a few minutes, or spend a couple of hours on a loop of 10 km or more – trails aren't marked, but you'd have to work hard to get lost. Popular spots get crowded, especially on summer weekends, but the further north you go, the fewer souls you'll be sharing it with. At its most northerly point, there are genuinely surprising views of Dublin Bay – panning from the hills of Howth to the Poolbeg Lighthouse and Pigeon House Towers. Look out here for container ships slowly squeezing between the walls into Dublin Port. The changing light, whipping wind and white-tipped waves make the sea seem almost painterly. It feels at once urban, and utterly wild.

North Bull Island's mix of habits – mudflats, sandflats, sandmarshes and dunes – are beloved of birds (and birders). In winter, tens of thousands of waders, wildfowl and gulls roost here – you might see Brent geese from the Canadian Arctic, as well as a short-eared owl or snow bunting if you're very lucky. Arctic and common terns begin to appear from April, and watch out for waders like oystercatchers, curlew and bar-tailed and black-tailed godwits in summer. Kestrels and Peregrine falcons can be spotted, too.

All of this diversity saw Bull Island named Ireland's first bird sanctuary in the 1930s, and is one reason Dublin Bay is today a UNESCO Biosphere Reserve. This small spit of land has 'the most conservation designations of any site on the island of Ireland', according to Dublin City Council. But balancing the sensitivities of fauna and flora with modern life and plentiful visitors is not easy. A climate and biodiversity emergency was declared in Ireland in 2019, and issues with traffic, litter and off-leash dogs are common – lots of birds nest or feed in the grasses, shingle and sands, so if you are a walker or dog-owner, do your bit by sticking to the trails (and keeping dogs on a leash).

MUCK ROCK

Pirates, warriors and stunning views

Howth, Co. Dublin
Howth DART station (5–10-min. walk); Dublin Buses 31 and 31a serve bus
stop 557 at Howth Road DART station, a short walk from the turn-off to
Howth Castle

Most hikers come to Howth head for the Cliff Path or Tramline loops. But beautiful as they are, there's another tramp that takes you to views that top the lot.

To access Muck Rock, walk west from the harbour and pass through the gates of Howth Castle. Dating in its current form from the 16th century, the castle has been home to the Gaisford-St Lawrence family for hundreds of years and runs a cookery school in the old kitchens. Tradition has it that Grace O'Malley, the pirate queen, landed at Howth around 1757 and called in at the castle in the hope of dining there and obtaining supplies. The gates were closed to her, however. Greatly offended, O'Malley abducted Lord Howth's heir and took him to Co. Mayo. He was returned on the promise that the gates would never be shut at dinner time and that a place would always be laid at the table for an unexpected guest. That extra place continues to be laid to this very day.

To get to the rock, continue to the Deer Park Hotel, following the golf course to the right of the building until the pathway enters the thickets of rhododendron at its base. This is easier at some times of year, and in some types of weather, than others (it's not for its cleanliness and ease of access that the hill is known as Muck Rock). As you walk, watch out for Aideen's Grave, a collapsed portal tomb dating from megalithic times, said to be named after the wife of Oscar na Fianna. Oscar, a legendary warrior, was the son of Oisín and Niamh (of Tír na nÓg) and the grandson of Fionn Mac Cumhaill. His death caused his grandfather to weep for the first (and only) time in his life, and Aideen to die of grief. Oisín is said to have built the tomb at Howth, the capstone for which weighs over 70 tonnes. It has long since collapsed, giving the appearance of a huddle of rocks, or some ancient husk.

Winding up the hill, you'll eventually pass through the leaves to a stunning view of Dublin Bay. On a clear day, you can see as far as the Mourne Mountains from here. Even in poor weather, you can make out the kitesurfers on Dollymount Strand and the Martello Tower on Ireland's Eye offshore. The tiny island can be reached via ferry from the East Pier, with a hidden beach offering one of the best picnic spots in the city, its stacks teeming with seabirds – including puffin, terns and guillemots.

Not a bad return for a walk up a muddy rock.

YE OLDE HURDY GURDY MUSEUM ⑮

E10MAR calling …

Martello Tower, Howth, County Dublin
sites.google.com/site/hurdygurdymuseum
May to October 11am–4pm, November to April (weekends only) 11am–4pm
Howth Dart station (5 to 10-min walk); Dublin Bus routes 31 and 31a serve
bus stop 557 at Howth Road Dart Station (10-min walk)

A hurdy gurdy may officially be a musical instrument, but ever since former Taoiseach Seán Lemass walked into the studios of Radio Eireann one day in the 1950s, asking the controller 'How's the hurdy gurdy?', it took on a life of its own.

Well, it did in the mind of Pat Herbert, anyway. Herbert was the man behind Ye Olde Hurdy Gurdy Museum, a fascinating collection of vintage radios and communications devices housed in a hilltop Martello tower in Howth. Having grown up in County Mayo, he traced his own love affair with radio back to an afternoon spent listening to the 1947 All-Ireland Football Final as it was broadcast live from New York. Collecting went on to become a passion.

On display are all manner of curios. Stacks of historic devices line the 2.4-metre-thick walls of the tower – a 1940s Marconi here, a 1920s crystal radio there. A Paris Aerial looks like a framed photograph of Rita Hayworth until it's turned around to reveal wires, dials and instructions for gaining reception. Based on an aerial designed by the French underground movement as an answer to Germany's jamming of BBC news bulletins during the Second World War, it went on to become a novelty household device. Other whimsical creations are designed to look like spice racks, chameleons or cars. There are beautifully retro TV and radio all-in-ones, old valve machines, a 110-year-old Edison phonograph and 1950s trannies made to look like ladies' handbags. Most spellbinding of all, perhaps, is the actual Heathkit Apache ham radio set that brought first word of the Niemba ambush to General Seán McEoin. On 8 November 1960, eleven Irish soldiers were ambushed by Baluba tribesmen while on peacekeeping duties in the Congo. Nine were killed, and news of their fate was delivered to the Chief of Staff on this very machine.

The Martello tower in which Herbert's collection is displayed also has its place in the history of Irish radio and communications. Lee De Forest, the American radio pioneer, experimented with transmissions here in 1903 and it later housed a Marconi station. Today, the tower and museum are home to an amateur radio station with the call sign 'EI0MAR'.

GEORGE IV'S FOOTPRINTS

King-sized boots to fill

West Pier, Howth
Howth DART station (5–10-min. walk); Dublin Buses 31 and 31a stop at bus
stop 557 at Howth Road DART station, a short walk from the West Pier

It's fair to say that history hasn't been kind to King George IV (reigned 1820–30). But then George IV wasn't exactly kind to history. 'One of the idlest monarchs ever to ascend to a throne,' is how Irish historian Turtle Bunbury puts it. From shortly after his birth in 1762, when the attending courtier declared him to be a girl, to his death in 1830, the king was variously described as lazy, inept, drunk, corpulent, absurd, vain, fitful, cruel, indulgent, dissolute, a national joke and an inveterate spendthrift.

In 1821, shortly after his coronation, George IV visited Ireland, where he is said to have staggered off the boat at Howth in a state of intoxication. He had apparently gorged himself on goose pie and Irish whiskey during the crossing, after which his landing footprints – pointy-toed and dainty of heel – were cast on the West Pier by stonemason Robert Campbell. From there, the king went on to wow the Irish population, as Bunbury writes, 'by drinking toasts, shaking people by the hand, and calling them all Jack and Tom … like a popular candidate come down upon an electioneering trip.'

Over 200 years later, the footprints remain on the pier – '16 paces in this direction', as a sign helpfully points out – and are regularly filled with rain and/or seawater. They barely hint at the catastrophes that preceded and followed the brief moment during which the casts were taken.

George was as renowned for his extravagant lifestyle as his disastrous marriage. In fact, his wife, Caroline of Brunswick, died just five days before he landed at Howth – though the monarch not only saw fit to continue with his travel plans, but remained abroad during her funeral. Pressing business included visiting his mistress, Elizabeth Conyngham, at Slane Castle. 'It is believed that the reason the road from Dublin to Slane is one of the straightest roads in Ireland is because it was so designed to speed him on his journey,' as Henry Conyngham, the Eighth Marquess Conyngham, writes on his website. To this day, the bedroom he slept in at Slane is known as the King's Room.

Needless to say, George IV is remembered almost wholly without sympathy. Although his visit to Ireland was a success, Robert Huish wrote in his biography of 1831 that he had contributed more 'to the demoralisation of society than any prince recorded in the pages of history'.

CASINO MODEL RAILWAY MUSEUM

An intimate, nostalgic and hypnotic little time capsule

Dublin Road, Malahide, Co Dublin
modelrailwaymuseum.ie
Tuesday–Sunday from 9.30am, Monday from 1pm; last entry at 5pm (April–September) and 4pm (October–March)
Dublin Bus routes 32 and 42 run from Dublin City Centre to Malahide (stops 3485 and 3635 are at the Cricket Club nearby); Malahide Dart Station is a 5-min walk away

In a world of touchscreens and mass production, there is something endearing about analogue treasures. And Cyril Fry's lovingly assembled collection of model Irish railway engines, wagons and carriages is that, and more. 'It's very easy to think everything comes out of a box nowadays', as Tara Manning, Supervisor at the Casino Model Railway Museum in Malahide, which showcases Fry's collection, puts it. These certainly did not.

Fry joined the Midland Great Western Railway in 1922, at the age of 17, later working as a railway engineer and draftsman at the Inchicore Railway Works and a Senior Engineer with CIE. You can see those skills in the exquisite accuracy of his drawings and models – built to precise scale, with wheels cast in his own moulds, models painstakingly painted and an abundance of ingenuity (one engine even puffed smoke from a funnel). A mock-up of Fry's desk gives a glimpse of his attention to detail in creating over 350 pieces, right down to matchboxes made into drawers to house the tiniest of screws. 'To do things like this, you have to be [meticulous]', says Fry expert, Jonathan Beaumont. 'There was no 3D printing in those days.'

The little museum is set in a thatched cottage that once served as Malahide Castle's hunting lodge (casino is Italian for 'small house'), and it also tells the story of Ireland's railways: there are displays, coats of arms (including the CIE's, nicknamed the 'flying snail'), brass name plates and more. One interactive display shows how much of the island was covered by a spider's web of tracks in rail's 19th-century heyday … and how little was left decades later. Fry's models take us from the earliest trams and engines through to the black and orange B141 diesel locomotives and carriages of the 1960s (he died in 1972). It's an intimate, nostalgic and hypnotic little time capsule.

One black and white photo shows Fry and his daughter Patricia in their attic in the 1950s, surrounded by his O gauge working rail display, regulated by a miniature automatic signal system. 'Whenever my father launched a new model, there was great excitement in the household', she recalled. The models you see running on the tracks today are not Fry's, incidentally (his are in the cases). After his death, his family asked that they never run again.

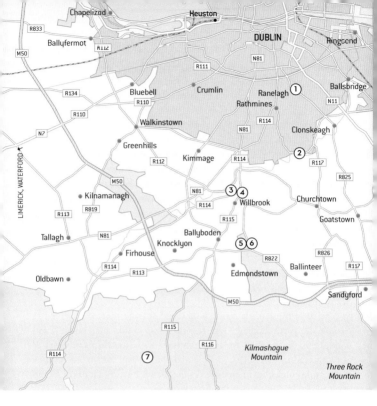

Outside the Centre – South

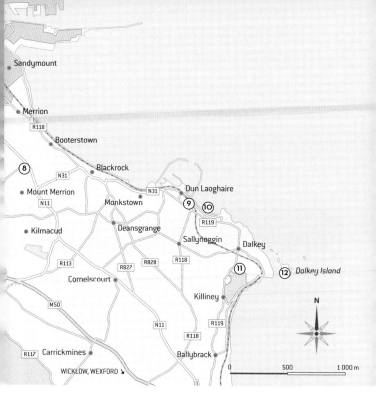

SITE OF IRELAND'S FIRST MANNED FLIGHT

Ireland's first aeronaut

Ranelagh Gardens, Dublin 6
dublincity.ie
10am until dark (5pm–10pm, depending on the time of year)
Admission: free
Luas Green Line stops at Ranelagh village, a very short walk from the
gardens; Dublin Buses 44 and 61 also stop nearby on Ranelagh Road

Think of aviation pioneers in Ireland and certain names spring to mind – the Wright Brothers; Alcock & Brown, who crash-landed in a Connemara bog after completing the first non-stop transatlantic flight in 1919; or latter-day disruptors like Ryanair's Michael O'Leary. But there is an Irish aviator who took to the skies in the late 1700s and whose first, unlikely flight helped pave the way for them all.

That man was Richard Crosbie (1755–1824). On 19 January 1785 (14 months after the world's first manned balloon flight had taken place in France), the 30-year-old from Baltinglass, Co. Wicklow, made history when he flew a homemade balloon over Dublin Bay. Crosbie's departure point was the newly developed Ranelagh Pleasure Gardens, and over 20,000 people are said to have watched the lift-off. 'The balloon and chariot were beautifully painted,' according to *The Annual Register*, 'and the arms of Ireland emblazoned on them in superior elegant taste.' Something of a showman, Crosbie's outfit wasn't far behind – 'a robe of oiled silk lined with white fur, his waistcoat and breeches were made of quilted satin, and he wore Moroccan boots and a Montero cap made from leopard skin'.

The 6-foot 3-inch (1.91m) aeronaut was sweating it, however. Having already made two failed attempts, 'he showed signs of acute anxiety during the preparations', as Brian MacMahon, author of *Ascend or Die: Richard Crosbie, Pioneer of Balloon Flight* (History Press Ireland, 2010), has written. But eventually, Crosbie managed to inflate the balloon with hydrogen and took off, floating over Merrion Square, swooping above the Custom House – which would have been under construction at the time – and eventually landing on Dublin's North Strand, near Clontarf.

His feat made Crosbie the first Irishman to complete a manned flight, but his larger goal – a pioneering balloon flight from Dublin to London – ultimately proved elusive. Today, you'll find a modest sculpture of the young dreamer, propeller in cap and paper plane in hand, created by artist Rory Breslin for this tiny, 1-hectare park hidden in suburban Dublin 6. In 1775, 5 hectares of pleasure gardens surrounded Crosbie as he took flight; today, Ranelagh Gardens feel a little like a deflated balloon.

THE DODDER RHINO

'We couldn't get a hippo'

Classon's Bridge, Milltown Road, Dublin 6
Dublin Bus stops 2817 and 2898 are a 10-min. walk away on Milltown Road,
near the intersection with Dundrum Road

The River Dodder is renowned for its wildlife. Gushing through Tempelogue, Bushy Park, Milltown and Donnybrook before joining the Liffey at Ringsend, it's possible to see otter, kingfisher, bats, brown trout and cormorants along its course. And, erm … rhino.

Or at least, one rhino. He's made of bronze, bolted to a concrete platform in the water just west of Classon's Bridge and shrouded in mystery. The sculpture is said to have appeared overnight in 2002, but nobody seems to have claimed responsibility or ownership (officially, at any rate). Staff at the Dropping Well pub, which overlooks the river at the junction of the Milltown and Churchtown roads, won't be drawn on the beast's provenance. 'We couldn't get a hippo,' was the cryptic response when Secret Dublin made inquiries …

The pub has, however, come up with a name – 'Woody' – apparently decided upon following a customer competition. The rhino has also been known to don a Santa hat at Christmas, so perhaps it's not completely outlandish to suggest a publicity stunt. Extinction does not appear to be on the cards either. Despite being knocked over by floods and having debris regularly festooned about his hooves, the Dodder Rhino recently celebrated his twentieth anniversary.

The Dropping Well itself was first licensed during the Great Famine in 1847 – not just as a pub, but a community morgue. During those years, a steady trail of starving and disease-ridden souls would have walked and communed along the riverbanks here, so twinning the two must have made sense to John Howe, the pub's original owner. Today, you'll find tables in the dining area with views over the river, a granite bridge named after John Classon (who built it and the sawmill that once stood on the site of the pub) and, of course, Woody the rhino.

BUSHY PARK'S NATIVE TREE TRAIL ③

One of Dublin's loveliest lungs …

1 Bushy Park Road, Terenure, Co Dublin
dublincity.ie
January 10am–5pm, February 10am–5.30pm, March 10am–6.30pm/7.30pm,
April 10am–8.30pm, May 10am–9pm, June and July 10am–10pm, August
10am–9.30pm, September 10am–8.30pm, October 10am–6.30pm/7.30pm,
November 10am–5.30pm, December 10am–5pm
Dublin Bus routes 15B, 16 and 17 stop at the Dodder Park Road and Dodder
Bridge; 15 and 49 stop along the Tempelogue Road

Bushy Park is one of Dublin's lovliest lungs, dotted with ponds and playgrounds, bordered on one side by the River Dodder, and laced with woodland paths that feel at times like deep countryside despite mostly being within earshot of the passing traffic. Depending on the time of year, you might find locals sunbathing on the open grass, squirrels hopping around autumnal woods, or frosty scenes with tunnels of dark branches seeming almost to scratch the skies.

What few people realise is just how many of the tree species here are native to Ireland, or the roots those species have in our culture, as well as our soil.

You can see them, and explore the park, by following Bushy Park's little-known Native Tree Trail, which charts a path between 15 native trees – including holly, hazel, apple, elder, alder, willow, oak and bird cherry (download a booklet and map in PDF form on dublincity.ie). There are plenty of fun facts along the way … did you know, for example, that the hazel supports some 73 insect species with food and shelter, or that hazel rods were used as early as 6,000BC to weave shelters and walls in Ireland? Or that the aspen is known as the 'whispering tree' because of the sounds its leaves make, or that yews give their name to Terenure – it comes from the Irish Tir an lúir ('the land of the yew')? Bring a crayon – when you locate the markers, you can make rubbings from them in the booklet.

Bushy Park itself dates from 1700 when Arthur Bushe, Secretary to the Revenue Commissioners, built the house known as 'Bushes House' here – it was sold to the then Dublin Corporation in the early 1950s. It's one of several city parks with surprising Native Tree Trails (others include Herbert Park, St Anne's and Markievicz Park), and is home to lots of other wildlife too – keen-eyed birders might spot herons, moorhens, swans, ducks, treecreepers and kingfisher.

RATHFARNHAM CASTLE

A fascinating fortified house

Rathfarnham, Dublin 14
01 493-9462
heritageireland.ie; rathfarnhamcastle.ie
Late April–late September: 9.30am–5.30pm daily
Late September–late April: Wednesday–Sunday 10.30am–5pm
Dublin Buses routes 16, 16A, 17 and 17A stop by Rathfarnham Castle

In 1912 Fr. Frank Browne was a Jesuit trainee and passenger on the RMS *Titanic*. He travelled out of Southampton on the first leg of the ship's maiden voyage, taking dozens of photographs that have gone on to become iconic records of the liner and its passengers.

He never got further than Cobh, however. Although Browne had been invited to remain for the full journey, when *Titanic* dropped anchor off the coast of Cork a brusque telegram from his Provincial was waiting. 'GET OFF THAT SHIP', it said: 1,517 passengers and crew went on to lose their lives, while Browne disembarked with his treasure trove.

That's just one of the fascinating facts popping up on a tour of Rathfarnham Castle, an unusual suburban heritage gem that just gets more intriguing the deeper you look. The castle dates from 1583, when it was built for Adam Loftus (1533–1605), the former Archbishop of Dublin, Lord Chancellor of Ireland and first Provost of Trinity College. It's probably the earliest example of a 'fortified house' built in Ireland. Such buildings, as the OPW's website (rathfarnhamcastle.ie) outlines, mark a significant stage in the transition from military castles to country houses in Ireland – going some way to explaining the castle's weird, hybrid appearance, which is further underscored by its lime rendering.

The original fortified building, with its flanker towers, was substantially remodelled by Henry Loftus, the Earl of Ely (1709–83). Further, 20th-century wings (now demolished) were added by the Jesuits, who bought the building in 1913, a year after the *Titanic* sank, using it as a seminary and retreat right up to the 1980s. Browne spent time living at the castle, taking many photographs of it (you can view some in the South Dublin County Library digital archive at source, southdublinlibraries.ie). Highlights of today's sparse, but beautifully restored interiors, range from original rococo stuccowork to 16th-century gun loops and sweeping spaces like the first-floor ballroom. Look out for a small passageway dubbed 'Apollo Sunburst Passage' – its ceiling is the work of William Chambers, while the roundels over the doors were designed by James 'Athenian' Stuart. This is the only house in Ireland where designs by the two can be seen in one place. The secret histories just keep on coming.

HUDSON'S FOLLIES

Robert Emmet's courting grounds

St Enda's Park, Grange Road, Rathfarnham,
Co. Dublin
01 493-4208
pearsemuseum.ie
November–January 9am–4.30pm; February 9am–5.30pm, March
9am–6pm, April 9am–8pm, May–August 9am–9pm, September 9am–8pm,
October 9am–6pm; From 10am at weekends and on holidays
Admission: free
Dublin Bus 16 stops opposite the park on Grange Road

Say the words 'park' and 'Rathfarnham' and one place comes to mind: Marlay Park has been a playground for generations of locals, hosting everything from buggy-pushers to summer rock concerts to hikers setting off on the Wicklow Way. But there's another park nearby – 33 hectares of greenery that are arguably more beautiful, and certainly more intriguing.

St Enda's Park was laid out in the late 18th century by Edward Hudson (1743–1821), a wealthy dentist with a practice on Grafton Street. He bought the property, christened it 'The Hermitage' and set about dotting the woodland paths with a unique collection of follies based on Irish field monuments. They are still there today. Follow the meandering trails through the trees, and you'll come across a hermit's cave, an Ogham stone, a vaulted archway, a ruined abbey and a stone watchtower. There's a faux hermitage, built from a jumble of stones in the eastern woodlands. Its doorway is locked today, but a room inside contains an arched recess and a stone bench, and a dolmen outside doubles up as a picnic table.

Such follies might be dismissed as an elaborate waste of money, of course – were it not for the romance of one particular local tradition. Hudson is said to have allowed the Irish nationalist leader Robert Emmet to meet secretly with his sweetheart Sarah Curran in the grounds (Curran's family lived nearby, and the avenue forming the northern border of the park is named after her today), so it's tempting to imagine the pair whispering amid the ruins. After their clandestine courtship, the couple became engaged in 1802, though their romance was cut short after Emmet's ill-fated rebellion of that year. He was captured as he attempted to visit Curran in Rathfarnham and subsequently executed – on a butcher's block.

That same block – so it is claimed – can be found in the Pearse Museum today. The museum is housed in Hudson's old mansion, which later became Padraig Pearse's home and boarding school for boys. Pearse renamed 'The Hermitage' as 'St Enda's Park' in 1910.

PEARSE BIRTHPLACE & MUSEUM ⑥

Schools and shopfronts

Birthplace: 27 Pearse Street, Dublin 2
Museum: St Enda's Park, Rathfarnham
01 493-4208; pearsemuseum.ie
Museum: November–January, Monday–Saturday 9.30am-4pm; February,
Monday–Saturday 9.30am–5pm; March–October, Monday–Saturday
9.30am–5.30pm; On Sundays and bank holidays, the museum opens at 10am
Admission: free
Birthplace: Pearse Street DART station (5-min. walk)
Museum: Dublin Bus 16 stops opposite St Enda's Park on Grange Road

Padraig Pearse (1879–1916) was one of the main leaders of the Easter Rising, but there's no statue commemorating him in Dublin. He's not alone – of the seven signatories of the Proclamation of the Irish Republic, James Connolly is the only one with a statue in the city centre. Pearse, however, is remembered in other places and ways.

Visit Glasnevin Cemetery and you might chance upon re-enactments of his oration at the graveside of Jeremiah O'Donovan Rossa ('Ireland unfree shall never be at peace …'). Stop at 27 Pearse Street, and you'll find a restored Victorian shopfront carrying the name of his father's stonemasonry business (Padraig and his brother Willie were born in the building, which today houses the Ireland Institute for Historical and Cultural Studies). Venture into St Enda's Park in Rathfarnham, and you'll discover one of the best small museums in the city.

The Georgian building at the centre of the park was Pearse's home for a time, and the setting for his bilingual boarding school for boys. St Enda's (or Scoil Éanna) began life in Ranelagh as a cultural nationalist experiment, using new methods of teaching Irish, literature, history, music, nature studies and physical education. It moved to Rathfarnham in 1910 and, a few cordoning ropes aside, it looks like the boys left only yesterday – an old dorm contains rows of iron-frame beds laid out under high ceilings, there's a sparse school chapel, and Pearse's study retains his desk and chair. Artefacts include a cannonball from the siege of Limerick, a print depicting the torture of Anne Devlin, historic swords and pistols, and even the gruesome butcher's block on which Robert Emmet is said to have been beheaded.

St Enda's was widely deemed a success, though not everyone was impressed with the way things were run. 'The regime in the school was strict, the living conditions were Spartan, and the food was scarce,' recalled one former pupil. It ran into financial difficulties before the Rising, although these were assuaged when donations piled in after Padraig, Willie and two other teachers were executed in 1916. The school finally closed in 1935.

THE HELL FIRE CLUB ⑦

A forest with a fright

Montpelier Hill, Dublin Mountains
dublinmountains.ie
Car park: 7am–9pm (April–September) and 8am–5pm (October–March)
The Hell Fire car park and forest entrance are situated about 6.5km south of
Rathfarnham on the R115 to Glencullen

Hell is the last place one wants to end up on a hike. But it's a very live possibility in the Dublin Mountains – if legends about Montpelier Lodge are to be believed.

The building, squatting eerily atop Montpelier Hill, was originally built as a hunting lodge by William Conolly, Speaker of the Irish House of Commons, around 1725. In his day, Conolly was the richest commoner in Ireland (his principal residence was Castletown House in Cellbridge, Co. Kildare) and he certainly picked his spot: the views from 390m above Dublin City and Bay are sensational. After Conolly's death in 1729, however, legend tells of the lodge coming to be occupied by 'wild young gentlemen' who had been barred from a tavern in the city. It's hard to separate truth from tradition at this stage, but the Hell Fire Club went on to earn itself a historical reputation as one of the most debauched dens of iniquity, gambling, drinking and satanism on the island.

The stories are legion. One suggests a Stone Age tomb was destroyed during the construction of the hunting lodge (during a recent archaeological dig, a rare discovery of megalithic art was made on a stone unearthed at the site). Others tell of dogs refusing to enter, of black masses, poltergeists interrupting late-night drinking parties, of the ghostly whiff of brimstone and the occasional appearance of the devil himself. The Hell Fire Club (motto: 'Do as you will') is also said to be haunted by a black cat, the ghost of a creature ritually scalded with *scaltheen* (a cocktail of whiskey and butter) back in its horrible heyday. One of the club's most famous members was Richard Whaley, who is believed to have gone even further, dousing a servant in brandy and setting him ablaze in 1740. In the ensuing chaos, the building caught fire, Whaley leapt out of the window and several drunken bucks lost their lives.

There's no doubt that Montpelier Lodge's reputation colours a visit. It's a blackened bunker of a building, seeming almost to crouch down in the grass. Inside, clammy walls are covered in ancient and modern graffiti, and floors are littered with piles of earth, twigs and broken glass. You can climb upstairs to the first storey, where fireplaces snake through the walls up into holes in the charred roof and metal bars protect the open windows. A visitor centre is in the works, but for now, the Hell Fire Club is definitely a day-time excursion ...

SPIRITUAL SIGNS

'This sign will change. God's love remains'

St Thomas's Church, Foster Avenue, Co. Dublin
01 288-7118
booterstown.dublin.anglican.org
Sun services (check website for times) are open to all
Dublin Bus stop 2009 and 2070 are nearby on the Stillorgan Road

Could these be the most thought-provoking traffic lights in Dublin? Set at the junction of Fosters Avenue and the N11 Stillorgan Road, a red light stops you beside a blue sign bearing a spiritual message with a difference. 'Seven days without prayer makes one weak,' it might read. Or: 'This sign will change. God's love remains.' Not long ago, motorists could have learned that 'When God saw you, it was love at first sight.'

Or what about: 'Jesus is my rock and I am ready to roll …'?

The sign belongs to St Thomas's Church, dating from 1874 and today run by the Anglican parishes of Booterstown and Mount Merrion. The church interior, which can be seen at morning mass on most Sundays, contains several features of interest – including a stained-glass window designed by Evie Hone. But the exuberant signs out front are what lodge most in the mind. 'The idea is to make people think, to give them a smile, to help them feel positive, encouraged or a bit upbeat,' explains parish rector, Rev. Gillian Wharton. The first sign went up in the 1990s and they're changed around once a year. 'Different messages have different aims,' Wharton explains ('Jesus the carpenter is looking for joiners' is her own favourite). 'We don't want to seem like we're proselytising – that's the absolute opposite of what we want to do. But the sign is in such a prime location that people will often drop in suggestions through the letterbox. We've even had people emailing [ideas] from overseas.'

The fun and creativity doesn't stop there. The parish holds a 'Sausage Service' in St Philip & St James' Church once a month, offering young people involved in Sunday sports the chance to worship quickly and informally before scooting over to the parish centre for sausages and potato wedges. A blessing of the animals takes place on the fourth Sunday in May, with parishioners bringing cats, dogs, rabbits, gerbils, guinea pigs, budgies, hens, hamsters and a host of other pets to the church to be blessed. 'Quiet Christmas' is another novel service responding to a need: held the Sunday before Christmas at St Thomas's, it's aimed at parishioners 'who do not want to do the whole razzmatazz thing' on the day itself.

Before you know it, the lights are green and you're on your way again.

SEASIDE BATHS

The original infinity pools ...

Blackrock, Dun Laoghaire, Sandymount, Clontarf
Blackrock Baths: Blackrock DART station (2-min walk); Dun Laoghaire
Baths: Dun Laoghaire DART station (10-min walk); Clontarf Baths:
Clontarf DART station (10-min walk); Sandymount Baths: Sydney Parade
DART station (10-min walk)

There's a fading bronze plaque by the railway bridge in Blackrock. It's half-turquoise now, in the way that only bronze can go, but you can still make out the inscription. It commemorates Eddie Heron (1910–85), for 35 years the undefeated diving champion of Ireland.

'His skill, grace and courage will never be equalled', the plaque states. A few steps below the bridge lies the derelict site of some of Heron's greatest dives. The Blackrock Baths, originally built in 1839 and for almost 150 years a magnet for bathing and watersports in the area, are today a crumbling ruin. In its heyday, this facility accommodated up to 1,000 spectators at swimming galas, diving contests, water polo matches and the Tailteann Games. But it has been abandoned since the mid-1980s and finally lost its iconic diving boards in 2012, when Dun Laoghaire-Rathdown County Council demolished most of the surviving structure because of safety concerns. Believers still hope the baths will reopen, but silted up, tagged with graffiti, worn down by wrecking balls and bashed by 'the ravages of the sea', that day seems further off than ever.

There's a similar story – albeit one with a happier ending – in Dun Laoghaire. The public baths there date from 1843; at their peak, they offered not just sea and freshwater pools, but children's facilities and medical installations using sulphur, seaweed and hot seawater (they're directly across from the Holy Hatch at Teddy's ice-cream shop). In recent years, a redevelopment has conserved the Baths Pavilion, cleared dilapidated structures and created a new jetty and walkway offering views of Scotsman's Bay … although no baths. For that, you can travel to Dublin's north side, where the recently restored Clontarf Baths feature a 900-square metre, five-lane seawater swimming pool – for details on events, lessons and public swimming sessions, see the Clontarf Outdoor Pool Facebook page (facebook.com/clontarfoutdoorpool).

Meanwhile, another hulk on Sandymount Strand looks least likely to be rescued. These sea baths were once linked to the coast by a 75-metre iron and timber pier, but all that remains today is a discarded husk of concrete, set adrift in the sand.

ORATORY OF THE SACRED HEART ⑩

A magical little mausoleum hidden behind a shopping centre

Off Library Road, Dun Laoghaire
dlrcoco.ie
Guided tours take place during Dun Laoghaire-Rathdown County Council's spring and summer heritage programmes
Dun Laoghaire Dart Station is a 10-min walk; Dublin Bus routes including 11, 46a, 63, 7, 75, 7a stop nearby on Clarence Street

I t reveals itself like a magical little mausoleum. Hidden behind a shopping centre, and within a shell building, the Oratory of the Sacred Heart measures just 6 metres by 3.6 metres. Visitors pause while a further cage gate and wooden doors are opened, before stepping into one of Ireland's great works of Celtic revival art.

At first, it's hard to know where to look. You almost feel the overall oomph of detail, colours and interlacing motifs before seeing the individual elements. There are swirling patterns and vibrant colours. There are birds and beasts that could have flown from medieval monastic books, intricate Celtic crosses, sober figures in stained glass windows by Harry Clarke Studios and surprising, zoomorphic creatures that wouldn't be out of place in a bedtime book by Axel Scheffler and Julia Donaldson. Every wall is covered in a richly immersive work that took 16 years to create. 'It's quite a delicate monument' as Deirdre Black, the Council's Heritage Officer, muses. 'She only used house paints.'

'She' was Sister Concepta Lynch (1874–1939), a Dominican nun also known to her family as Lily. The oratory was built as a memorial to local men killed in the Great War, but this little-known artist spent several hours a day, often in cold, poorly lit conditions, enhancing it beyond anyone's expectations. Between 1920 and 1936, she sent instructions to the local hardware store for her paints (the Dominicans were a closed order), mapped out her designs, cut stencils, and painted freehand onto the cement walls. It's a Celtic revival time capsule that feels spiritual, but contains hints of Byzantine art, fantasy and at times even nods to Pointillism and Art Nouveau. The methodical, carefully calculated approach is absorbing, but somehow also feels carefree and wild.

Lily took some inspiration from her father Thomas Lynch (1852–1887), the heraldic artist and illuminator. She spent much time with him, was encouraged to study Celtic art and manuscripts like the Book of Kells, and ran the business for several years after his death when she was just 16. The oratory itself looked destined for dereliction, languishing for several years after St Mary's Dominican Convent was sold in 1991 and replaced by a shopping centre and cinema. But a drive to protect it and fund its restoration and surrounding peace garden was successful, and today those who take the time to visit reap the rewards. 'I've been here thousands of times', as James O'Sullivan, Heritage Properties Officer, puts it. 'But I always see something different.'

THE METALS & DALKEY QUARRY

In the footsteps of funiculars

Dalkey Avenue, Dalkey,
Co. Dublin
Dalkey DART station (10-min. walk); Dublin Bus stops 3057 and 3058 are a
5-min. walk away on Ulverton Road. Routes 7d, 8 and 59 serve the area

Driving along Dalkey Avenue, it's very easy to miss The Metals. One reason for this is the disconcerting name: what sounds like an industrial site, or a sculptural installation, is in fact a thin little footpath. Slicing through this leafy suburb, its granite slabs are the only clue to a history that has left an indelible mark on Dublin Bay and the city streets.

The Metals are the former route of a funicular railway. Built in 1817, the system was designed to transport granite from Dalkey Quarry to Dublin Bay and, at its peak, 250 wagonloads of stone traversed the 3-mile (4.8km) distance every day. Each train bore about 18 tonnes of rock in three wagons, with empty trucks hauled back up on a parallel line, and horses taking over for the final stretch to the harbour. By 1823, some 1,000 workers and their families were living in the area and the village had 37 pubs. Conditions were not as salubrious as the modern-day suburb might suggest, however – many workers lived in cabins without running water, there were outbreaks of cholera, and dangerous work 'led to many losses of eye, limbs and even lives', according to an information sign. The results of their labour, however, remain on magnificent display today – in the harbour, the flagstones of Dublin's streets and as far afield as the Basilica of St John the Baptist in St John's, Newfoundland.

If you follow the laneway up to the quarry itself, it's still possible to see marks made by the chains in the great granite slabs. That isn't all. The views from the hilltop are amazing – stretching from Dun Laoghaire harbour past the South Bull Wall towards Howth (both the harbour and the wall were built using stone from this spot). Venture into the old quarry itself, and it's like walking through a miniature National Park. In sunny weather, granite crystals sparkle underfoot and climbers crawl all over the sheer slabs rising up from the earth.

Quarrying at Dalkey ended in 1917 and today the land forms part of Killiney Park.

DALKEY ISLAND

The 'thorny island'

Dalkey, Co. Dublin
Dalkey DART station (10–15-min. walk); Dublin Bus stops 3057 and 3058
are a 10–15-min. walk away in Dalkey Village

It's like a reverse Alcatraz – an island lying just 300m off the coast of South Dublin, so close you're tempted to dive off the pier and swim across. Nobody does, however, because the postcard-pretty Dalkey Island lies on the other side of a treacherous sound.

There are ways and means of getting there, of course. In summer, local fishermen can be hired for the return journey out of Coliemore Harbour. Kayaking companies also run guided tours from Bulloch Harbour, paddling out over surprisingly clear waters to explore the Martello tower, St Begnet's Church and an old gun battery on the island. Although measuring just 25 acres (some 16 hectares) in size, Dalkey Island hosted some of the first Stone Age settlers on Ireland's east coast, and artefacts like arrowheads, axes and pottery have also been unearthed, pointing to

Neolithic and Bronze Age activity. One excavation of a Neolithic midden even found the skeleton of an adult male whose skull had been filled with periwinkle shells. Strange as it may seem, Dalkey Island (the literal Irish translation of 'Deilginis' is 'thorny island') has also been used for farming.

The island's Martello tower and battery date from 1804, when they were built as part of a broader system of coastal defences against Napoleonic invasion. The garrison remained here long after the threat passed – in fact, the British military is said to have paid soldiers for many years 'for their idleness', during which time they integrated into Dalkey society, marrying local girls, raising families and keeping goats, as an information sign reveals. St Begnet's ruins date from the 10th century (the little church is named after an Irish princess said to have fled an unwanted suitor to embrace Christianity in Britain). The island is also home to tern colonies and populations of wild goats, rabbits and brown rats. The most exciting wildlife to spot on a visit, however, are the local dolphins and seals, which can regularly be seen playing about in the sound – one of the most biologically diverse areas on the east coast. Prison never felt so free.

ALPHABETICAL INDEX

Thomas Jonglez

It was September 1995 and Thomas Jonglez was in Peshawar, the northern Pakistani city 20 kilometres from the tribal zone he was to visit a few days later. It occurred to him that he should record the hidden aspects of his native city, Paris, which he knew so well. During his seven-month trip back home from Beijing, the countries he crossed took in Tibet (entering clandestinely, hidden under blankets in an overnight bus), Iran and Kurdistan. He never took a plane but travelled by boat, train or bus, hitchhiking, cycling, on horseback or on foot, reaching Paris just in time to celebrate Christmas with the family.

On his return, he spent two fantastic years wandering the streets of the capital to gather material for his first 'secret guide', written with a friend. For the next seven years he worked in the steel industry until the passion for discovery overtook him. He launched Jonglez Publishing in 2003 and moved to Venice three years later.

In 2013, in search of new adventures, the family left Venice and spent six months travelling to Brazil, via North Korea, Micronesia, the Solomon Islands, Easter Island, Peru and Bolivia.

After seven years in Rio de Janeiro, he now lives in Berlin with his wife and three children.

Jonglez Publishing produces a range of titles in nine languages, released in 40 countries.

ACKNOWLEDGEMENTS

Over the several editions of this book, the author would like to thank Claire Connolly, Catherine McCluskey (Fáilte Ireland), the OPW (with special thanks to Catherine O'Connor, Patricia Ryan and Dorothea Depner), Dublin Civic Trust, Dublinia, Deirdre Black and James O'Sullivan (Dun Laoghaire-Rathdown County Council), The National Museum of Ireland, Dublin City Council, Harriet Wheelock (RCPI), The National Gallery of Ireland, Dr Jason McElligott (Marsh's Library), John Mahon (Lucky's & The Locals), Liam Finegan (Iveagh Trust), Dr. Mary Clark and Leo Magee (Dublin City Archives), Rhona Delaney, Denis McIntyre, Rev. Gillian Wharton, Paul O'Kane (formerly of Dublin Airport), Jana Gough, Robert Poynton, Niamh Connolly, Prof. Annraoí de Paor, John McKeown and Éanna Rowe (Waterways Ireland). The author also wishes to thank Lynnea, Rosa and Sam Connolly, without whose love and patience this book would not have been possible.

PHOTOGRAPHY CREDITS

All photos by Pól Ó Conghaile, with the exception of 14 Henrietta Street (14 Henrietta St / Ros Kavanagh); Bull Island (Fáilte Ireland / Gareth McCormack); Custom House Dublin & Casino at Marino (OPW), Stained Glass Room (Collection: Dublin City Gallery The Hugh Lane), Goya's Portrait of Dona Antonia Zarate (National Gallery of Ireland), Windmill Lane Recording Studios (Windmill Lane Recording Studios), Metro Burger Sign (Lucky's) and the Old Terminal Building (courtesy of Dublin Airport).

Maps: **Cyrille Suss** – Layout: **Emmanuelle Willard Toulemonde** – Proofreading: **Jana Gough, Sigrid Newman and Kimberly Bess** – Publishing: **Clémence Mathé**